a -to- gen Z CROSS WORDS

72 PUZZLES THAT *HIT DIFFERENT*

ADA NICOLLE

PUZZLE WRIGHT PRESS

New York

PUZZLE
WRIGHT
PRESS
New York

An Imprint of Sterling Publishing Co., Inc.

42 of the puzzles in this book originally appeared on www.patreon.com/luckyxwords
from October 2020 to May 2023.

ISBN 978-1-4549-5265-7

For information about custom editions, special sales, and premium purchases,
please contact specialsales@unionsquareandco.com.

Printed in Malaysia

2   4   6   8   10   9   7   5   3   1

unionsquareandco.com

Cover design by Erik Jacobsen
Cover illustrations by Autumn Studio/Shutterstock.com (flower);
Martyshova Maria/Shutterstock.com (smiley face, lines);
ivn3da/Shutterstock.com (pencil)

CONTENTS

INTRODUCTION

Hi! I'm Ada. I grew up solving and creating crosswords. I absolutely loved playing Scrabble as a kid. I loved it so much I bought graph paper and started spending my time intersecting words, which endlessly fascinated me. From there I discovered crossword puzzles, and I got hooked. Alongside that, I grew up with pop culture, the Internet, and a brain obsessed with finding patterns. It took a while, but I eventually realized I could combine it all.

I'm also gay! In 2021, I came out as a queer trans woman and named myself "Ada" as a tribute to my love for crossword puzzles. (ADA is a common piece of crossword fill, with 600+ appearances in the New York Times crossword alone.) It's something I'm proud to be. I'm here, I'm queer, and I'm using the clue [___ of corn] for EAR.

This book is a collection of a variety of things that bounced around in my head between 2020 and early 2023: "Am I trans? (Yes.) Has anyone ever noticed this thing? (Yes.) That's a good song, I should take note of that. (Please validate my music taste!)" These crosswords' contents range from song lyrics to film stars, phrases picked up in conversation to weird facts picked up online, callbacks to throwbacks. It's the fun stuff I noticed was fifteen letters long—a typical puzzle's size—and references I thought were important/fun/ridiculous enough to include. It's an homage to the Internet, without which this book wouldn't be possible. It's got a sense of humor, from which, as a Canadian, I have to drop the "u" for this book.

Long story short, crosswords are my form of poetry. I like taking all the things in the world I find interesting and storing them in boxes for the world to see. It's now up to you to break them open.

I hope, even if you're not a regular crossword solver, you can find some joy in this book. I can't promise these puzzles won't be a challenge (jk they definitely will be), but I think it's worth it. Take your time, and feel free to ask a friend for help. Treats are sometimes best shared :)

Enjoy the puzzles!

—Ada Nicolle

1

ACROSS

1 Genre blending old jazz aesthetics with modern drum kits
13 "Easier than you thought, eh?"
15 Measurement for some transfems
17 Fudd of old cartoons
18 Descriptor for the "Five" from "Queer Eye"
19 "<3" equivalent, in texts
21 "___, Felicia"
23 ___ Lanka
24 Uses, as a hip-hop beat
26 Expensive sports cars, casually
28 Booking prices
30 Old theatre type whose "nickel" variety is the namesake of a children's network
31 "They destroyed us out there"
32 Singer Erykah
33 Language group including Xhosa and Zulu
34 Sign-___ (YouTuber outros, e.g.)
38 Listings in a character bio
40 :
41 Part of a "Wipeout" course
44 Grow older
45 Haudenosaunee people
46 Boat paddle
47 "Beats me," online
48 The "Me" in "Despicable Me"
49 Bro, sis, etc.
51 Spoke (up)
53 Like the principles of communism
58 Handheld fusion food with nori and rice
59 "Feeling's mutual!"

DOWN

1 Ada's mom in 2021's "Lamb," e.g.
2 Word before "Vegas" or "Palmas"
3 Of great renown
4 ___ + Alt + Del
5 ___ Reuters (Toronto-based company)
6 Hype parties
7 Cheri of "Saturday Night Live"
8 Info on a U.S. tax form
9 Snarf (down)
10 "The mic's working"
11 Website menus with links such as "FAQ" and "Home," for short
12 High school diploma alternative, briefly
14 Place for a not-so-famous celebrity
16 Fruit that doesn't sound so fast?
20 Model ___ (some school clubs)
21 Amoeba's form
22 When repeated, "blah blah blah"
25 Tushie
27 Contraction referring to the immediate future
28 Al ___ ("to the tooth")
29 Secondary accounts, casually
31 Cry loudly
33 Problem for a sitter?
35 Gender quality for some genderqueer people
36 F-150 producer
37 Slithery animal, in memes
39 Ingredient in 58-Across, often
40 Steering wheel or transmission, e.g.
41 "woah!!"
42 When doubled, a Pacific island
43 Ostracizes
44 ___ d' (headwaiter)
46 Poppy product
50 "___ oui!" ("But yes!," in French)
52 Timothée's role in "Call Me by Your Name"
54 Nickname for an Egyptian child king
55 Sports org. whose players stay in their lanes?
56 Phillipa of "Over the Moon"
57 School based in Houston, for short

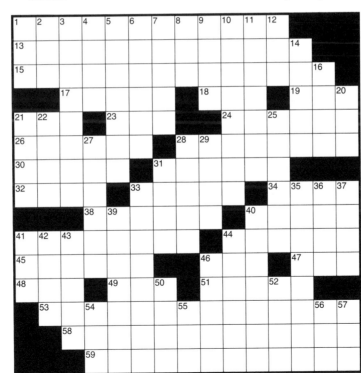

ANSWER, PAGE 79

2

ACROSS

1 Comedy posters?
10 Boat that anagrams to cattle
14 Start of a post–"Happy Birthday" chant
15 "Not a chance!"
16 "Mock the Week" or "QI," e.g.
17 Stun
18 What 21 is not, for 9 + 10
19 Lady (and not a laddy?)
20 "Results may ___"
21 Sea in sad time-lapses
23 "Have a nice TRIP, see you next ___"
24 Supportive communities, affectionately
30 Protection from Canadian winters, for many
31 "Mr. Roboto" band
32 How garage sale items are sold, typically
34 Country that could hypothetically be pronounced like a Jar Jar Binks pronoun

35 White-and-yellow flowers
38 Word before "Spice" or "Cube," in rap names
39 Pettiness
41 ___ fine (have no apparent issues)
42 Powered and pedaled transport
44 "This means so much to me, really"
47 Uber calculations, briefly
48 Norwegian home to the Viking Ship Museum
49 Fedoras and fezzes, e.g.
50 Depiction on Amazon.com

52 "The Peacock Network"
55 "Love Island" setting
56 Way to the very top?
59 Scoop
60 Prolonged occurrence at film festivals, often
61 Vyvanse treats it: Abbr.
62 Make a coherent argument

DOWN

1 Sentient "Dora the Explorer" object
2 Periods of a discography
3 Where "GF" often means "gluten-free"
4 Preventer of dark circles

5 Office-seeker, informally
6 System used by deaf people Down Under
7 Split the bill, cutely
8 Name that anagrams to "nose"
9 Does embroidery
10 Country on the Gulf of Aden
11 King whose reign started September 8, 2022
12 Like melted cheese
13 "SmackDown" org.
15 Adjective for some officers
22 Take one's turn in class, maybe

23 Prix ___
24 Essential computer components, briefly
25 Tackles
26 Dentists recommend you maintain it
27 Isolating way to be lost
28 Early hit for Evanescence
29 Go ___ mode (flip out)
33 Noticed
36 Succumbs to curiosity
37 Say convincingly, as a lie
40 Was a snitch
43 Dessert akin to a brownie
45 Like Squidward's voice
46 "You're so much better than me"
49 Rear
50 Group of players
51 Naan flour
53 German city that straddles the Rhine
54 ___ in the machine
55 By means of
57 They're usable after being burned
58 Salmon product

ANSWER, PAGE 79

3

ACROSS

1 Jump in the pit, perhaps
5 Allows in, say
13 Relative of a cardigan
15 Nintendo series whose first installment was subtitled "Mega Microgame$!"
16 "I heckin' agree!"
18 Meme word associated with an upward arrow
19 Potato ___
20 jeffdunham.com, e.g. (or when pronounced as a word, the name of his puppet that he uses to make jokes about "kids these days")
23 Unlike wet paint
24 Comic artist Olive ___ Brinker
25 Made some noise for Elon Musk
27 Manual format, often
30 TD Garden athlete, informally
31 Response to "You're not gonna get away with this!"
35 "Just say no" speaker

38 Aftershow segment, often
40 Combine
43 Space to unwind
44 Love to see
45 Comedian Edebiri
46 Tampa Bay player, briefly
48 Rest after a long morning, maybe
49 Restrict the movement of
52 Slow to play
55 Resilience despite previous challenges
60 Some household fire hazards
61 Where x = 0
62 Olympics aren't usually held in them (except once in Tokyo)
63 Cursed cereal-eating utensil

DOWN

1 Artist featured in YouTube's "Rewind YouTube Style 2012"
2 "I get it!"
3 Parent to three "gorls," in a film franchise
4 Not just mine
5 Peppermint ___ (winter treat)
6 Array at a drink table
7 Red dot appearing on one's forehead, e.g.
8 Where to meet emus in your area, maybe
9 Popular dog costume among "Star Wars" fans
10 The Beaverton's genre

11 ___ cake (inedible item)
12 Collection in a stationery section
14 Takes a profound turn
15 Crave
17 Many a furry girl
20 Program that guarantees money for citizens, briefly
21 Word before "side" or "show"
22 ___ Bunny (Bugs's crush)
26 Messed with the wrong guy, say
27 Construction sign?
28 Batted but didn't field, for short
29 "The ___ Monster" (Lady Gaga album)
30 Coughed up

32 Unlike rainforests
33 Spoonful, perhaps
34 Insatiable quality
36 One of the social sciences, briefly
37 Croft of video games
39 Something apparent in one's step, sometimes
40 Hawaiian "thank you"
41 Something seen when nothing else is
42 Loch known for a song rather than a monster, which I guess is also cool
46 Prepares for delivery, maybe
47 "This sucks"
50 Teeny
51 "Put comma inside quotes", e.g. [hehe]
52 Way out there
53 Array at a buffet table
54 "Once Upon a Snowman" protagonist
56 ___ diavolo sauce
57 Prefix for "planet"
58 Christmas tree option
59 Nonverbal disapproval

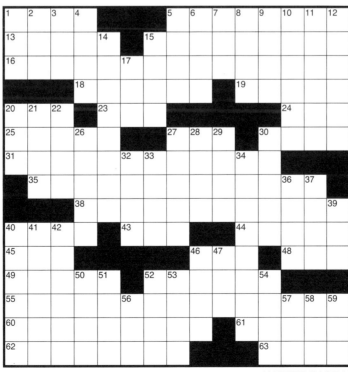

ANSWER, PAGE 79

4

ACROSS

1 It's built upward
6 Downtempo music genre also called "chillhop"
10 ___ Philadelphia (where the Fresh Prince spent most of his days on the playground)
14 Piercing hook
15 Felt bad, like an insult
16 California roll ingredient, casually
17 Now possible to follow
19 Show off every angle of an outfit
20 Confidentiality doc, briefly
21 Have a small amount of
22 Was ___ (got played)
23 Word after "1000" or "10,000," in hyperpop album titles
25 Derrick Johnson's org.
27 Went out in, say
28 Dwayne Johnson's role in "Moana"
30 Like double entendres
32 Building site?
36 Stereotypical vlog soundtrack
37 Act that "nobody likes," per an IDKHow song (they change a word to "headlining" at headlining shows)
38 Response to "Do you want your glasses?"
39 "I'm just a pig!"
42 Prefix for "izm," on singer Erykah's debut album
43 "I. Am. ___." (Lightning McQueen catchphrase)
47 Products of mint facilities?
49 Knuckle tats, e.g.
50 Relative of Enrique
52 Nova Scotia neighbour, briefly
53 Spoke thus:
55 Webkinz product
57 Taro root relative
58 Accented movement?
59 "___ Wafer Top Hat Time" (Rhett & Link song)
60 Accessory for a bride-to-be
61 Tomorrow's expert, today
62 Word before "star" or "verse"

DOWN

1 Felt bad, like an insult
2 Biking option
3 Animal with Suri and Huacaya breeds
4 "___ blimey!"
5 Like many sweaters
6 Capital found in a dog breed name
7 Leavin' (here)
8 Go up without a hitch?
9 "___ be my honour ..."
10 British cans
11 Beyond blissed
12 Its poles get very cold
13 Paid attention (to)
18 ___ Houten ("Simpsons" surname)
24 Secondary drop-down
26 Part of PNG
27 "Our mission was a success"
29 Some hotel amenities
31 Binary type of question
33 Wall-climbing plants
34 Person dominating in the game Actorle, e.g.
35 ___ stand
36 Cocomelon-obsessed toddlers, likely
37 Daily air in Ontario public schools
38 Birds associated with Thoth
40 Gatorade bottle part, often
41 Goes down a considerable amount
44 Like an unexplainable glow
45 Put in a field, e.g.
46 Gru's brother in the "Despicable Me" movies
48 Occupy, in a way
51 Bowen of "Saturday Night Live"
54 "What was I thinking, Marge??"
55 Group among which only one in the U.S. has been married to a "second gentleman"
56 Watson portrayer on "Elementary"

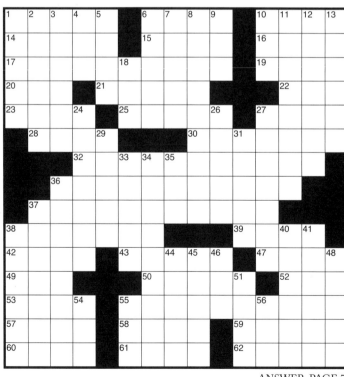

ANSWER, PAGE 79

5

ACROSS

1 Self-inserts in fan fiction, say, briefly
4 "Miracle Workers" network
7 Bothers
11 Unbelievable experience
13 Cuzco's country
14 Accomplishment
15 Not for here
16 Window parts
17 "___, Not ___" (romance novel by South Asian author Sonya Singh)
18 Oodles
20 Levy of "Schitt's Creek"
21 Toronto Raptors shout
23 "Check it out!"
24 See 28-Across
25 "I'll take that as ___"
26 Steals, cutely
28 With 24-Across, 15-second spots, often
31 Works on a story?
32 Byzantine structure built in the 6th century
33 Establish permanently
34 ___ beans
35 End of a presidential address?
38 "Mrow" alternative
39 All-encompassing
43 Guac ingredient, casually
44 Devastating superlative
45 Disaster relief org.
47 Three-card game
48 Many of them were latchkey kids
49 Part of < or >
50 They're mined by crafters
51 Swagger
52 PS5 producer
53 Like 69
54 Trudeau and son, e.g., briefly

DOWN

1 Trudeau's birthplace
2 Said with pride
3 Google Maps listings
4 Saxophone type
5 Musical comedian Domino
6 Venting in "Among Us," say
7 Some worries
8 Like some uneditable files
9 "Carpool ___" (James Corden segment)
10 Has visible lines over it, maybe, in comics
12 Tigger's friend
13 Unskilled prizefighters
16 University Park campus
19 Tries to eavesdrop, say
22 Sway rivals, in TikTok drama
23 October 1st baby, e.g.
27 Like Cheerios compared to Froot Loops and Frosted Flakes
28 Name that can fill in the "Odd Couple" episode titles "The ___ Games" and "___ the Influence"
29 Duolingo event of 2021
30 Breakfast treats that some people freeze
31 Reddy hit that became an anthem for second-wave feminism
32 Dismissal
33 5-Minute ___ (notorious content farm)
35 "Such Great Heights" is its second track
36 Modern way to reach out
37 Feature contributions, often
40 .puz file content, briefly
41 Sharpened
42 What "T" means, in image editing software
46 ___/all
47 "I got beef"?

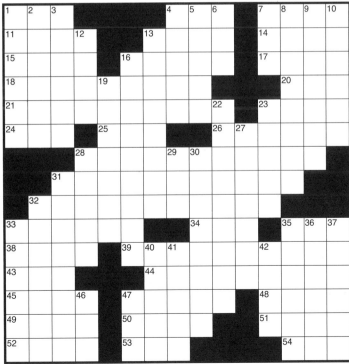

ANSWER, PAGE 80

6

ACROSS

1 Watson's company
4 Parental ___
8 Food designed to withstand climate change, e.g., briefly
11 Canadian clothing chain whose name sounds more fitting for a coffee chain
13 Became harder to ignore
14 uBlock Origin for Chrome, e.g.
16 Zack and Cody's home, in a Disney Channel show
17 Business deal offered in l33tspeak, probably
18 Sites of environmentally unfriendly extractions
20 Animal with a prehensile nose trunk
22 ___ your boot (haul ass)
23 Leave in a hurry
26 Request that artists probably LOOOVE
30 Portmanteau term for teen-centric programs
33 Something highlighted on a test, maybe
34 Grab-and-go staple
37 Boring, as a party?
38 Lemony moniker
39 ___ Beanies ('90s collectibles)
41 Composed
43 "You ___ hand it to 'em ..."
46 Bygone Russian rulers
48 Long overdue, say
53 Do as you're told
54 Stinks
55 "Given that context ..."
57 Electricity unit
58 Distributes
59 Stop, as a livestream
60 Abbr. associated with sudden listlessness?
61 Letters implied on Canadian street signs

DOWN

1 "Don't take me seriously," jokingly
2 Freight train part
3 Crossword with a second layer, e.g.
4 Coffee container
5 Super Smash Bros. character in a red cap
6 "Really?"
7 ___ hammer (Mjolnir)
8 Unwelcome sight from that friend who "told you so"
9 Typo-correcter's meat substitute?
10 Has debts
12 Trans medication option
13 What plucky sorts might pursue?
15 Vaping additive, for short
16 Something unpacked at a campfire
19 Pea container
21 Turnarounds?
24 Improv inits. since 1990
25 Contents of a kid's treasured chest?
27 Cash in on cultural relevance, maybe
28 Comfy shoe, briefly
29 "La-da-dee-da-da-dee-da / On the st___-___-___-___-o" (lyric in "Pump It" by Black Eyed Peas)
31 Abbr. omitted from "Do the Dew"
32 Support, as a couple
34 Placed (down)
35 Having four sharps
36 Prefix for "ATM," in phone-recycling fixtures
40 When "Phinéas et Ferb" takes place
42 Drafted, as a document
44 Know Your Meme article?
45 Wise words
47 Many a GarageBand instrument, for short
48 "I'm walkin' here!"
49 Thick Japanese noodle
50 Very far away, say
51 Fan's montage set to music
52 ___Cup (period piece?)
56 Name that sounds like the start of a question in French

ANSWER, PAGE 80

7

ACROSS

1 People "serviced" in some media
5 Princess Fiona, e.g.
9 Store
13 Group of star players
15 Brand whose name means "to hit a target" in Japanese
16 Satisfied pregnancy cravings
17 Gray rain clouds
18 "Magic" Mr. Clean product
19 Page finish, maybe
20 Mohawked fool-pitier
21 Ask invasive questions
22 "Of COURSE"
23 One ___ time
25 Where to take someone who was in a "peek-a-boo accident," in a joke
27 Edible component, sometimes
29 Become the focus
36 Jingle heard between episodes of "SpongeBob," perhaps
37 "Damn right, girl"
38 Opposite of WNW
39 Become inedible
40 udel.___ (palindromic University of Delaware URL)
41 May and Abe, for two: Abbr.
43 Subject of a high school brag, maybe: Abbr.
45 "This is so unlike ___"
47 Trash collector, in Australia
49 Grimm fairy tale character
51 Ring-shaped reef
52 It's made to be recognized
56 Stuck on with a UHU Stic
57 Boards
58 Depression nickname, with "the"
59 Model Holliday
60 Raid target

DOWN

1 Supervisor of caffeine products, e.g., for short
2 ___ house film
3 Formerly, in names
4 Harder to advise against
5 Another, in Spanish
6 Plays the fool on a 2000s prank show
7 Less honed by formal training
8 Atlanta university
9 Some high heels
10 Scottish woolen cap
11 Spheres
12 Consoles compatible with Wheels and Nunchuks
14 "The Addams Family" matriarch
15 Upset!!! >:(
20 "We're counting on you"
23 Part of ADA: Abbr.
24 Nevada/California lake
26 "___ n'est pas une pipe"
28 Not made using practical effects
30 Groups of players
31 "I don't need to know that"
32 They might be met with applause
33 Diner booking, slangily
34 "They're saying 'Boo-urns! Boo-urns!'" speaker
35 Color whose name means "unbleached"
42 Fully convinced
43 Stop talking to
44 Copy partner
46 Nudge
47 Shows distaste
48 Aang's show, for short
50 Weakens
53 de Armas of "Ballerina"
54 "___ been real"
55 Thrifting find

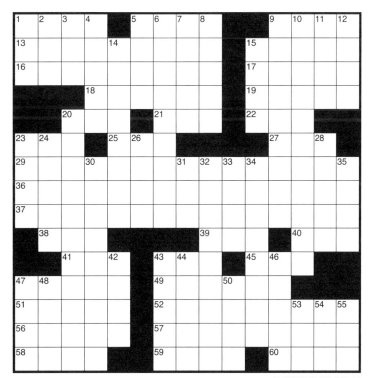

ANSWER, PAGE 80

8

ACROSS

1 Genre for many a Tony Hawk game soundtrack
10 Get up, stand up
15 Plug line
16 One-named Brazilian footballer
17 The original ending of "The Shining" et al.
18 Dos for Diana Ross and Pam Grier
19 "Pshyeah, sure"
20 Uses data abroad
22 Light
23 "This article is about the food. For NBA player nicknamed Beef ___, see Isaiah ___art" (Wikipedia disclaimer)
25 RenFaire refreshment
27 Setting for "Get'cha Head in the Game," in "High School Musical"
28 Split (up)
31 Smooth like butter
33 Format for '90s-era children's movies
36 Units calculated in a USD-to-MXN conversion
38 What Jughead in "Riverdale," as a self-proclaimed weirdo, doesn't do (and doesn't want to)
39 "Oh, soOoOorry!"
42 Said thanks for the shearing, maybe
43 ___ harvester (phrase similar to, but very different from "___ic farmer")
44 Susan of "L.A. Law"
45 Avery alternative
47 Timelines, e.g.
49 "when are we leaving?"
50 Hatha ___
52 BTS rapper who also goes by "Agust D"
55 Like Lisa of Blackpink
57 Volts times amps
60 Cutting vegetables, e.g.
62 Resonates, as a joke
64 "Star Wars" enemy, familiarly
66 Spaceship Earth's theme park
67 Spared no expense
68 Short period
69 Ukiyo-e and others

DOWN

1 Opera career highlights, maybe
2 Collection in a hardware store display
3 Clarity for a speaker, e.g.
4 Turned into a body of artwork?
5 Toronto street described as "not a nightmare in this city," on BlogTO
6 Jury member
7 Command that won't affect saving a file
8 Often-misquoted "Star Wars" line
9 Artist Otis ___ Kye Quaicoe
10 "I ___ Lost Boy from Neverland ..." (lyric from Ruth B.'s "Lost Boy")
11 Tennis's Nadal, to fans
12 Flushed out
13 Vlog genre involving gossipy personal anecdotes, e.g.
14 It's not hard to make
21 Comedian Vulcano
24 Clean water off, say
26 Redirects resources from
29 Bother
30 Photo app whose aesthetic includes Hydroflasks
32 Soldiers, for short
33 Bugs on the road?
34 iPhone feature with a step tracker
35 Mosh
37 Knight of Death Row Records
40 Surname of any Zach who I once put in a Twitter group named "Ex-Zach-___!" (sorry about that)
41 Oman neighbor, briefly
46 Plant, as a seed of doubt
48 Equip (with)
51 Whittaker's successor on "Doctor Who"
53 SpongeBob's station at the Krusty Krab
54 Brand associated with American Eagle
56 Cult leader, e.g.
58 Cheap shelter
59 Things in brackets
61 Rollerballs, e.g.
63 Cardinals, on a scoreboard
65 Gamer's playing surface, perhaps

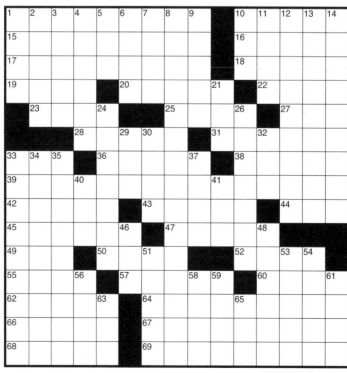

ANSWER, PAGE 80

9

ACROSS
1 Captain of the Pequod
5 Surrealist who had a pet ocelot
9 Cinema-celebrating nonprofit
12 Common source of (plant) estrogen
13 Empower, in a way
15 Anagram of salt's composition
16 La petite ___ (French euphemism for "orgasm")
17 Drinky time
19 YouTube mid-roll, e.g.
21 They may appear in callbacks
22 Avoid, as responsibilities
24 Where Tony Hawk debuted the 900
25 "Dungeons & Dragons: Honor ___ Thieves"
27 Anagram of salt's "composition"?
28 Show exhaustion, maybe
31 Like good catchers?
35 "___ idea was this?"
37 Small battery type
38 Many transport trucks
39 Undetectable changes to a Reddit post, e.g.
42 "Cool!"
43 To whom Hamilton says "You're an orphan. Of course! I'm an orphan"
44 "I got this"
46 Cute li'l lunch spot, maybe
48 Happen over and over, as a dream
50 "I am making this SO obvious right now"
52 Release
55 Element in Ultron's outer shell, in the comics
57 Trick
58 "___ anarchy is loosed upon the world" (pretty goth Yeats line)
59 Reached
60 Watches the years pass by, say
61 What a mess!
62 The source of the quote in 58-Down, e.g.
63 Color sources in TikTok videos, often

DOWN
1 Green fixtures
2 ___ earrings
3 Hairstyles for Kaepernick and Badu
4 Take cover?
5 Bit of morning wetness
6 Oscar-winning "Moonlight" actor Mahershala
7 Let have
8 Mountaineer's tool
9 Couples might plan it
10 Battles
11 Signs, as a contract
14 Caps Lock key, e.g.
15 Not negative about one's impact on the planet?
18 Gets hold of
20 Purpose
23 Make biscuits, like a cat
26 Hard-to-find collectible, say
28 Destr0y, as a n00b
29 Fish that looks like a greeting?
30 Umbrella term for many gender identities
32 Provide platters
33 ___ Rail (Canadian rail company with an ambigram logo)
34 Approx.
36 Kitt who voiced Yzma
40 Making a boo-boo
41 New parent, maybe
45 Black Widow's domain, briefly
46 Popular bathroom cleaner?
47 #1
49 Red, as vin
50 Some cured meats
51 "Oye Cómo Va" songwriter Puente
53 Like GOOS paper
54 "Ocean's Twelve" role
56 People of the Great Basin

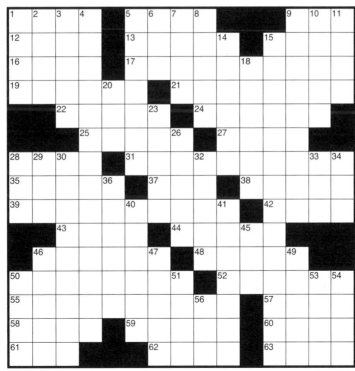

ANSWER, PAGE 81

15

ACROSS

1 What enemies are often at
5 "No worries"
15 Time to give up, for some
16 Branded sweater that zips up over the face
17 Berry with a cedilla
18 "You NEED to hear this"
19 Red, orange, yellow, etc.
21 "Don't ___ the Pigeon Drive the Bus!"
22 Mauve relative
23 DJ/future space tourist Steve
26 Subway saxophonist, e.g.
29 Side dish with gochugaru
33 Compound words break down into them
36 Smoker's residue
37 Spanish pronoun
38 Feeling really silly about, say
40 Onetime member of music's "Big Four"
41 Crumple up and throw away
44 Hoity-toity to the extreme
47 "Enough!"
49 They keep on tough faces
50 Eight, in German
52 Fakes left, say
54 ___ Dial-Up (Internet service provider)
57 Candy with a "Level Up" variety
61 Purpose of temporary passwords
64 Smooth, with "over"
65 Eco-friendly fast food offering
66 Letters describing some monitors
67 Viola Davis achieved it in 2023
68 Boomers, e.g.

DOWN

1 "In Summer" singer, on Broadway
2 Window decoration
3 Collection studied in genome research
4 Struggling to fall asleep
5 Common pairing with Estradiol, casually
6 Come (from)
7 Lhasa ___
8 "Neon" fish
9 "Don't worry about her"
10 Large gathering of fans, briefly
11 Like fresh "goss"
12 Any BTS member, e.g.
13 Cherry pairing, in some sodas
14 Language for many secure passwords
20 It's encouraged to avoid credit card fees
24 "___ ora" (Maori greeting)
25 Hits up, in a way
27 Birds that flap their wings while running
28 Keeps under control
30 Hacky, as a bit
31 Manmade borders
32 "___ something I said?"
33 Many baby foods
34 It might be enough
35 Little brat
39 "You'll wanna hear this!"
42 Romance author Huang
43 Abbr. often prefixed with "BI"
45 Patreon level
46 Gross, to a toddler
48 Elevated form of an often-overlooked pronoun
51 Letter that resembles an Estradiol pill
53 Didn't lose
54 Brood
55 Sweater-on-door handle problem
56 ___ baby (child with the advantage of a celebrity parent)
58 Feeling bad
59 "___ Wood sawed wood" (start of a tongue twister)
60 Salmon and others
62 Its full name means "Festival of the First Morning of the First Day"
63 D.C.-based org.

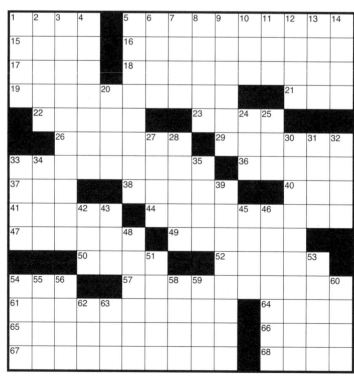

ANSWER, PAGE 81

11

ACROSS

1 Cartoon character with a jaguar companion
6 Carne ___ (Mexican dish)
11 Networks that are welcoming of new partners?
14 December 1st purchases
16 Property claims
17 Shares takes on Twitter, e.g.
18 Makes a goof
19 Uber-specific targeted ad offerings, often
20 Corporate money manager, briefly
23 Week, in Spanish
26 ___ d'Alene, Idaho
28 Shot that was nailed on the first try, in film slang
33 Kashi, as opposed to Lucky Charms, e.g.
34 Like the person who has everything
35 Orchestra woodwinds
36 Little Miss Muffet's seat
39 Sci-fi phaser sound, jocularly
40 Cheese that's wheel-y good (I am so sorry)
44 Activity performed in Ariana Grande's "34+35" ;)
45 Much of Saskatchewan
47 Mediterranean island country
48 It might explain the unchanging nature of energy or mass
52 "You'll need to take that up with somebody relevant"
53 Electrical unit namesake
54 Shallot relatives

DOWN

1 Places to cuddle up and watch movies, maybe
2 Opposite of EXT, in a script
3 Florida theme park inspired by Walt Disney's _xperimental _rototype _ommunity _f _omorrow
4 Flip out
5 Basic skateboard trick
6 Promgoer's woe
7 Soapy bubbles
8 Imitating, on menus
9 Hamburger's article
10 Bottom
11 Archaic word for "two days from now" (opposite "ereyesterday")
12 Pays tribute, in a way
13 Desires
14 Home-brewing products, often
15 Not looking too good
20 University of Northern Iowa town
21 Gas or food, e.g.
22 Hockey's Bobby
24 Klingon ___ (nickname for salamanders that look like the "Star Trek" species)
25 2, for He
26 Greek island that anagrams to C-FOUR
27 Just a small sample
29 Fanfiction settings, briefly
30 Canadian speed measurement, briefly
31 Prefix for "feminism"
32 Expressed sorrow
33 Zach Woods's role on "The Office"
34 ___, skip, and jump
37 "Something's Got a Hold on Me" artist James
38 Become less icy
40 Open mic establishments, often
41 Compete against
42 Unable to speak, maybe
43 Businesswoman Lauder
45 ["Over here!"]
46 Padmé Amidala's daughter
47 Discord overseers, briefly
48 Toronto-based news channel
49 "Gotcha!"
50 It's nothing, I swear!
51 Splatoon "ammo"

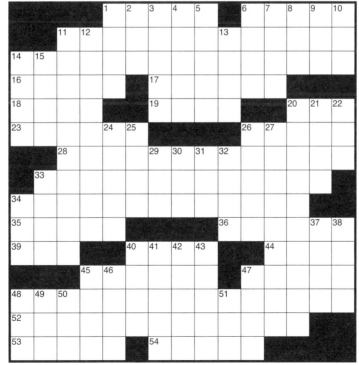

ANSWER, PAGE 81

12

ACROSS

1 Many a Pinterest album
10 Age ___ (18+ website feature)
14 Couple who's constantly making up?
15 It might start with "What do you call ...?"
16 Appeased, as an audience
17 Emcees
18 Look up to
19 "Perhaps that is the case ..."
21 "Is that what you wanted from me?"
23 Been horizontal
24 1,000,000, casually
26 "A ___ flew around my room before you came" (Frank Ocean lyric)
28 In fifth grade, likely
29 Left to wither, as plants
33 Dull paints
37 Words before a demonstration
38 Ranges
42 Request for personal information, in old chatrooms
43 Group from which Pluto got "plutoed"
45 Plant in topical creams
46 Body ___ (self-acceptance movement, casually)
49 "Don't go too hard on me"
51 University-oriented course, briefly
53 Cattle identifier
55 Represented, with "for"
56 Mystery Inc.'s Mystery Machine, for example
59 Hair dyes
60 "Stuf"
61 Shows up the entire class on, say
62 "Are you from ___? Cause I'd put U and I together ... wait, I think I screwed that up"

DOWN

1 Comedy show requirement
2 Progressive Ilhan
3 Chose to receive, as a newsletter
4 Austin Powers's enemy
5 Word often stretched out in the childhood complaint "I'm ___"
6 "That was SO last year"
7 Appended
8 Dearth of cluing ideas for yours truly, e.g.
9 Leading to a cruel fate
10 Render unwatchable in Canada, e.g.
11 On the blue
12 Bantu-speaking people
13 Printer brand whose commercials feature Shaq
15 Unlikely to initiate conversation
20 In the slightest
22 Miner discovery?
24 Fixtures sometimes also called "bankomats"
25 ___-ghetti and spag-balls ("American Dad!" dish)
27 "Of God," in Latin
30 Bagful at a breakfast diner
31 Canadian gas brand
32 Ration (out)
34 They introduce story arcs, often
35 Part of a conger line?
36 Attempts
39 You only get this, per Eminem's "Lose Yourself"
40 "I didn't ___ you as that type of person"
41 Become harder to climb
44 Secure, as a helmet
45 Members of a plural system
46 ___ fazool (Italian dish, casually)
47 Word before "nerve" or after "fiber"
48 Café offering
50 In a ___ (very quickly)
52 Break stuff?
54 Codenames or Catan, e.g.
57 Unpleasant feeling to evoke
58 Word before a maiden name

ANSWER, PAGE 81

13

ACROSS

1 ___ Halloween (chain that possesses old storefronts, aptly)
7 A public humiliation might begin one
15 Anderson of "Baywatch"
16 Harry Styles hit that starts with "Walk in your rainbow paradise"
17 James Baldwin pieces
18 Playlist contents for a BFF, perhaps
19 Something in everything
20 Mackey of "Barbie"
21 Doesn't assume, say
22 Distraction on a road trip, maybe
24 Crunchyroll offering
25 "Misery Business" genre
26 Give it back!
28 Obviously very hot
29 Change, as brain chemistry
32 Palindromic Pokémon that isn't Girafarig or Ho-Oh
34 Turbo and Smoove Move, e.g., in "Turbo"
36 Shoppers Drug Mart alternative
39 Figure played by Snoop Dogg in an Epic Rap Battle of History
41 Outperforms, in a sense
43 Dept. whose website has a "Where's My Refund?" page
46 Houston football team
48 TikTok's main feed, briefly
49 Occupy Wall Street sights
51 Going-out attire?
54 Stash
55 "___ the front door!"
56 "A Little Late with ___ Singh" (2019–21 NBC show)
57 It can't miss
59 "L'chaim," literally
60 Range rover?
61 Worrying sight for a 60-Across
62 Cool down
63 "Heck yeah," e.g.

DOWN

1 Open mic necessity
2 Break things?
3 "Let's DO it"
4 Paper measurements
5 "<3 <3 <3" alternative
6 Some Zoom call co-hosts, nowadays
7 Basmati alternative
8 It may depict a line with a bunch of zeroes
9 ___ Blend (Java Monster flavor)
10 Unit on a workout machine, maybe
11 Played again
12 63-Across at sea, maybe
13 Falco's request to Amadeus
14 Swore
20 Lindley of "Dispatches from Elsewhere"
23 "... lest I figure out what to do otherwise"
24 Echo assistant
27 Opposed (to)
30 "Who do you think you are? ___!" (confusing cry of triumph by bowler Pete Weber)
31 Hoots
33 "Don't just pick at your food"
35 Their toys aren't for all ages
37 Call for help?
38 Unwavering supporter
40 Greets respectfully
42 Most nimble
43 "What a pity"
44 Adjust for microtonality, perhaps
45 Features of some laughs
47 Domain suffix for Ookla's Speedtest
50 Contribute to public discourse, maybe
52 Tricks
53 Tricks
55 Sneak, e.g.
58 Camera letters after "D"
59 "From ___ Streets 2 ___ Suites" (2021 Snoop Dogg album)

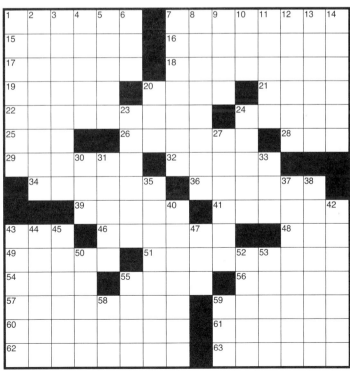

ANSWER, PAGE 82

14

ACROSS

1 Dial-up alternative
4 Person texted on the reg, likely
7 Secondary plot, in writers' room lingo
13 Yearly Christmas purchase for some
16 Of the eyes
17 Pictures in Instagram comments, e.g.
18 "___ home!" ("Come to papa!")
19 After Eight alternative
20 Namesake of a chess player's rating
21 Initials for some oils and gummies
22 Move in a circle
26 Comedian Sanders
27 Genre for the "America's Funniest Home Videos" theme song
29 Teensy
30 Places that don't require much commuting
35 "Oh hi!"
36 Improv comedian's question
37 Like dead-end Wikipedia links
38 Present, as a question
39 Abbr. for a chord with a perfect fourth
40 Wikipedian, e.g.
43 They may have jingles
44 Contraceptive method
45 "The Matrix ___" (2003 film)
50 Pasta dish, to a toddler
53 "That sounds like fun!"
54 Piña ___
55 For curative purposes
56 Knows the secret of, say
57 "Looking for," on dating profiles
58 Show that originated MacGruber, for short

DOWN

1 "Fiddlesticks!"
2 Makeout ___
3 Educational YouTuber Green
4 Feature of challah bread
5 Office plant, maybe
6 "The Book of Boba ___"
7 Friend at the corner store, maybe
8 Like pangolins
9 Henry VIII, e.g.
10 Word that some replace with "young"
11 Beam
12 Most of them were BCE
14 Navigators on the road, e.g.
15 Mansa Musa incorporated it into the Mali Empire
23 1986 James Cameron film
24 Levels of a wedding cake
25 "Who ___ could it be?"
26 Nickname for a famous Princess of Wales
27 Adjective in many car commercials
28 They're jingled for babies
30 ___ and dined
31 Thor or Loki, e.g.
32 Whimpers, say
33 "The deed has been completed"
34 K
35 Truth alternative
41 Saturn's largest moon
42 Put to shame
43 "Remembered" thing
45 "Pon de Replay" artist's nickname
46 Milk sources
47 Low platform
48 Surname that becomes a first name when an M is appended to the front
49 Haunted toy in some horror movies
50 "Poli" or "comp" follower
51 Round enders, for short
52 ___ Lilly (company whose stock plummeted in 2022 after a fake Twitter claim that "insulin is free now")

ANSWER, PAGE 82

15

ACROSS

1 Initialism whose last letter is sometimes replaced with an S
5 Syllable re___ed after "re" in Selena Gomez's "Love You Like a Love Song"
9 Bad mood
13 It'll usually stick to one side upon twisting (and MIT scientists are trying to figure out why)
15 ___ guys
16 Needs more
17 "The Last of Us" character
18 Specialists to call about bug issues
19 Contents of a personalized playlist, often
21 Abbr. under "Lucasfilm," in its logo
22 Robert of "Airplane!"
23 Like the acid commonly used to stain wood
25 "Woof"
29 How jokes probably shouldn't be taken
31 Show where fashion from France is often featured, casually
33 Prefix for "media" or "pedia"
34 Concept associated with lower stress levels and increased productivity
37 "You're on my hair!"
38 Got bubbly
39 Staying relevant?
41 Not able to move as much, say
42 Radical queer movement, for short
44 Imply
47 Real ___ (non-arts pursuit, to doubters)
48 "Barnyard" cow voiced by Kevin James
50 Attacked, kamikaze-style
52 "___ think that" ("Vouch")
54 Require follower requests, say
56 It'll get the word out
57 As a rule
58 PetroCanada alternative
59 With, in song titles
60 Carter of "Gimme a Break!"

DOWN

1 Spelling often seen on TV
2 "Amen"
3 Gossipy gal
4 Be led astray
5 Subject of a teenage proposal parents won't feel weird about, likely
6 "Grody to the max!"
7 Opposite of "odio"
8 Box office failure/fifth-highest-grossing film of 2020
9 Word before "de Janeiro," in skincare
10 Didn't validate
11 Meme-inspired baking show hosted by Mikey Day
12 Prepared to start driving, with "up"
14 Didn't mesh
15 "Check one of these two boxes" options
20 Person who gets things on a platter
24 "And that ties the score"
26 Package with preportioned ingredients
27 Maisie Williams role in "Game of Thrones"
28 "Fire belly" amphibians
30 Shaggy's "It Wasn't Me" collaborator ___ Rok
31 Good lines
32 Rocky Mountains park named for a Cree expression of awe
34 ___ fighters (WWII term for UFOs)
35 Points to the other side?
36 Literally, "fortress inside a city"
40 Single-masted boat
43 Unlikely hypothetical
45 Informed
46 Babyish?
47 Sailing maneuver
49 Loudness unit
50 Lie awake, maybe
51 Looking away, for many
53 Bingability concern, briefly
55 Sports org. founded in 1916

ANSWER, PAGE 82

16

ACROSS

1 Grody
7 Oona of "Game of Thrones"
14 Beauty brand touted by Jennifer Aniston
15 Powering, as a Bentley
16 Start transitioning, in a sense
17 Precede
18 Drops off some letters?
19 Word rhymed with "master" in Vampire Weekend's "Step"
20 Tech behind a Jugs gun
21 Audio accompaniments
24 Transmission component?
27 One-masted boat
29 Screensharer?
30 Lines of Python, e.g.
31 Like wholesome male celebrities, according to memes
36 "Ods bodkins!", e.g.
37 SoCal football team, briefly
38 "Study Finds Falling to ___ and Screaming to Sky Remains Best Way of Forsaking One's God" (Onion headline)
40 "Little Red Book" ideology
41 Shows like "Squid Game" and "Crash Landing on You," e.g.
43 Spidey sense
47 Favre known for football and for having a surname pronunciation that makes no sense
48 Descriptor for a pretty lady, in Spanish
49 Edit in post, as an early YouTube video
52 DJ name-dropped in "I Took a Pill in Ibiza"
53 Snitched on
54 ___ regions
55 Animals who gobble and also get gobbled
56 They'll take a wet load

DOWN

1 Origami requirement
2 Piercing location, for some (eeeek)
3 Lackluster
4 "For God's sake, not everything in life is like Hogwarts!!"
5 Something shared among club members
6 Accomplishes
7 Makes aware
8 Becomes more intense, with "up"
9 "Island" author Huxley
10 Group of DID systems
11 Freshness
12 Stat a QB wants to keep low
13 The Wikimedia Foundation is one: Abbr.
15 Adjective on some Goldfish packages
22 Weaving machines
23 7UP, e.g.
25 Sport ___ (all-purpose vehicle)
26 Avoided danger, say
28 Part of PPAP, in a viral music video
29 Gave an academic shout-out
31 Utensil for cooking chicken, often
32 Offensive
33 People of China and Vietnam
34 "Pressure" singer Lennox
35 Strongly affect, like an emotion
39 "If you're lonely when you're alone, you're in bad company" speaker
40 Photo finishes
42 Substantial
44 Crossword puzzles for me, e.g.
45 Mid
46 Epilator targets
48 Superfruit, e.g.
49 "This is ___"
50 New, in German
51 Broadcaster with a wine club: Abbr.

ANSWER, PAGE 82

17

ACROSS
1 "Let's blow this ___ stand!"
9 Gloria in "Madagascar," e.g.
14 "Community" college
16 Relative you aren't born having
17 DS-1 Orbital Battle Station, familiarly
18 Care Bear action
19 Portuguese direction
20 Unlikely, as a chance
22 Name that reverses to a common verb
23 Webseries where historical figures diss each other, for short
25 Baller settings
27 Twitch annoyances
32 Chicago paper, for short
33 Fae/faer and ey/er/em, e.g., casually
34 Flail on the video game controls as fast as possible and hope for the best
38 Brooding, say
39 Address to loved ones
40 Drag to court
41 Set of powerful moves, in gamerspeak
43 Go up some decibels
44 €
45 Ready for court, say
47 Stop and go?
49 ___ Cruces
50 Krueger of Nickelback
51 Twelve in the day
54 Italian fashion capital
58 Entered with haste
60 Old Met outfit?
62 Implores
63 Options in some software start-up menus
64 "Rome" rapper
65 Request after an impression of a friend, maybe

DOWN
1 Computer key with an "up" counterpart
2 ___ O's
3 Apple equivalent, in "iCarly"
4 Crossword makers, in Britain
5 Possible response to "Where are you?"
6 Purchases for players?
7 Lower back muscles, casually
8 Airline whose meals are entirely kosher
9 Alternatives to nods
10 Meantime
11 Vegan, say
12 City intended to end with the same vowel sound as "Emily," in a Netflix series title
13 Needed to give back, say
15 Tim's partner in comedy
21 Mobil product
24 Tiny ears
26 Catering containers
27 Once again
28 Game preview, briefly
29 GIF-like Instagram story posts
30 Singular praise, jokingly
31 Wineglass parts
35 Forbidden-sounding perfume
36 Enterprise inhabitant
37 Common menu header
39 Extra
42 Pair of hangers?
43 Bit of self-assurance
46 Steamed Mexican dish
47 "The Lorax" antagonist Aloysius who shares his name with an airport
48 Chimney sweep's covering
50 "Aw, ___ "
52 Controversial newspaper article, often
53 Common name for a pet clown fish
55 Getting points deducted, say
56 Tippity-top
57 Wooden bowl for eggs?
59 Surveillance org.
61 Record stat

ANSWER, PAGE 83

ACROSS

1 Tracking device chip
5 Source of extra hotel charges, often
12 ___ Beauty (cosmetics chain)
13 Its time is now!
14 Takes to go, say
15 "Dope"
16 First human in Maori mythology
17 Revelation in a moody drama, maybe
18 They may have stout sections
20 Jean-___ Picard
21 Trunkfuls?
22 Part of "GBBO," on the telly
25 "Refrain from commenting," on TikTok: Abbr.
26 One or two
29 C_6H_6
33 Bits
34 Came into one's own
35 ICU coverage?
36 "Spider-Man: Turn Off the Dark" co-composer
37 Make hostile
42 Texter's "tsk tsk"
44 Symbol next to a pronoun pin, maybe
45 "Stop stalling!"
48 Sharp shoot?
49 Street food with fried potatoes and chutney
50 The Weeknd's first name
51 Comedic breaks between rhymes
52 About
53 Entertainment center centerpiece
54 J.R.R.'s trilogy

DOWN

1 Vibrantly red gemstones
2 Word on some fish packaging
3 She's all the rage
4 ___ Racist ("You Oughta Know" group)
5 Some mobsters
6 Troubles
7 Inventor of dynamite/ namesake of Peace Prizes (!!)
8 They're chilling
9 Inhumane zoo fixture
10 Hathaway of "Ocean's 8"
11 Leftovers, e.g.
13 God with the head of a hawk
15 Sweetened, in a way
16 "Coming soon," on a schedule: Abbr.
17 Canadian comedian ___ Smith
19 Computer attachment
23 Mitchell of a classic Nickelodeon sitcom
24 Urgent care locations, briefly
26 Body mod, maybe
27 Getting the hell away, with "out"
28 Truffulas in "The Lorax," e.g.
29 Consumer protection org.
30 Chess rating system
31 Some long flights
32 Online show organizer, maybe
37 "La donna è mobile" and others
38 Guy bragging about Web3 and "stacking apes," e.g.
39 Angel's div.
40 Someone seamingly working?
41 Logo for getcracking.ca, aptly
43 Frickin'
44 "___ be ideal"
45 Have a quick back-and-forth?
46 Norwegian king name
47 Like Oreos that rob you of creme
50 "It's why no one watches ___ Blast" ("I Think You Should Leave" line)

ANSWER, PAGE 83

19

ACROSS

1 Percy Jackson, e.g.
8 Actor Taylor who married a Taylor (Dome) in 2022 after dating a Taylor (Swift) in 2010
15 Vividly purple Filipino dessert
16 How we hope aliens might arrive
17 True, despite sounding jokey
18 Brief rest on a road trip
19 Pencil that isn't used on paper
21 Workers with hods
22 Day on Mars
23 Nature Valley bar spillage
25 On the ___ (frequently)
27 The sentient utensil in "Toy Story 4," e.g.
28 Site for a Harley/Joker scene, in "Suicide Squad"
31 Longish skirts
33 ___ on the head
34 Tweety one, cutely
35 "Oh no you won't!"
38 E.E. Cummings, e.g.
39 Vibe with
40 Admonish
41 Some Twitter stats, briefly
42 Types
44 Emoticon before "what's this?"
45 Totalling
47 Really liked
49 Quiet mumble
52 Waxy space
55 Restricted
57 "Here's my theory …"
58 Snow White's sister, in a fairy tale
59 Emergency fund, maybe
60 Birds also known as "fish eagles"
61 Gets ready to go, say

DOWN

1 2021 Timothée Chalamet film
2 Some TikTok house residents
3 Rocks from the heavens
4 "Listen to me next time!"
5 "Vivo" character who has, appropriately, a way with words
6 Approving
7 Scares away
8 ___ stain (makeup product)
9 Its first book's cover depicts a boy turning into a lizard
10 Rise in pitch while speaking
11 "Bad Ideas" singer Violet
12 Intl. military alliance
13 Class that might study crypto (or a hyphenated description of crypto, to its detractors?)
14 Shows off, as merch
20 It's fought by opposing lines
24 "High" time
26 Part of a Tumblr "set"
28 Places for special treatment
29 Unfit for much plant life
30 Hashtag on an old Instagram pic, maybe
31 Like some points
32 Weaver of "Alien"
34 They're projected with one's breath
35 Media org. that's also a currency code
36 Michael who portrayed Allan in "Barbie"
37 Green opening
42 Knight-in-training
43 "It's Been Awhile" rock band
45 Bit of glowing coal
46 DoorDash delivery
48 ___ the room
49 Artist Joan
50 Some, in Spanish
51 Crooner's quality, maybe
53 Suffix for "camel" or "sPoNgE"
54 ∧, for a stick figure
56 They're sober for transportation reasons: Abbr.

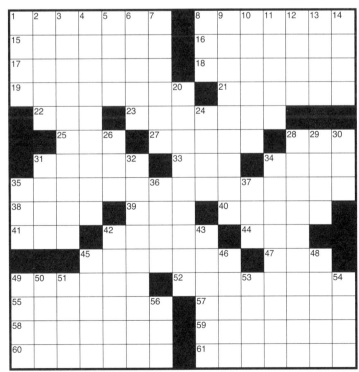

ANSWER, PAGE 83

20

ACROSS

1 One-upped
7 "That's pretty mid"
10 Teenager at a children's soccer game, often
13 Stop telling onstage, as a joke
14 Number that can be at most 340
17 Attach, as a certain patch
18 Soft slipper
19 Title for Mr. Cumference in "Pac-Man and the Ghostly Adventures"
20 Small drink
22 The Mighty Mighty Bosstones, e.g.
23 Not go bad
25 Pro at a desk, say
27 Bordeaux bud
28 Big ___ ("All Night" rapper)
30 Show weakness
32 Ms. Steele of a 2011 bestseller, familiarly
34 Chip variant with one extremely spicy chip in every handful
40 2014 Bleachers hit with an aspirational title
41 Like beards or dresses, for many
42 Patel of "The Green Knight"
43 Fifth note of a major scale
44 Part of XXX?
45 Xe/___ pronouns
47 Danny Brown genre
49 Abbr. akin to XXX
52 Honey in a jar, e.g.
56 Bout enders, briefly
58 Something for the course?
59 How many sports events are presented
61 Emergency broadcast, maybe
63 Be an inconsiderate guest, say
64 Sam of commercials, e.g.
65 Music center?
66 Sucked in, so to speak
67 Mentally prepares (oneself)

DOWN

1 Energetic
2 Like haunted house sound effects
3 Cheap option in many retailers
4 Sardine container
5 Feeling that reverses to a way to feel
6 Canadian tuxedo material
7 ___+ (network formerly known as Epix)
8 Counterpart of Thanatos, to Freud
9 Very, slangily but self-censoringly
10 Activist Parks
11 Baby name that means "Ireland"
12 Ward (off)
15 Many a cybersecurity warning
16 Lemon Demon song about a person who turned into an arcade machine
21 Toot
24 Proud pocket protector wearer, stereotypically
26 Tend to
29 Frustrated response to "Not good enough"
31 Received criticism (for)
33 Room at the top
34 "Check it out. Vibe it. Really, really ___ on it, and then, remember that feeling" ("Radio Rebel" line that became a TikTok meme)
35 Fall behind
36 Boat propeller
37 Latin for "where"
38 Pitchfork rating whose most recent recipient was Fiona Apple's "Fetch the Bolt Cutters"
39 Unit of the work force?
46 ___ ray
48 They often accompany puppy dog eyes
50 Like significant flaws
51 Some songbirds
52 Sheet of ice
53 Cozzie ___ (amount required for basic necessities, in Aussie slang)
54 Part of YSL
55 Very kewl
57 Catch
60 It'll change the locks
62 Expected, as a submission

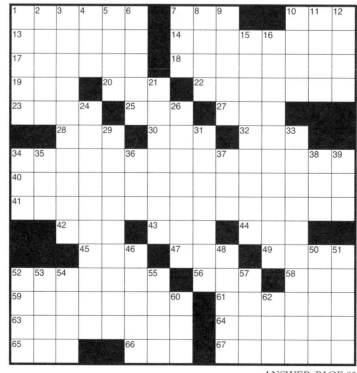

ANSWER, PAGE 83

21

ACROSS

1 Response to a jokey "Wake up sheeple!," maybe
4 ___ milk (soy or oat product, informally)
7 Gendered term for a firefighter, e.g.
12 Ariana Grande album with the single "Into You"
15 Their views are public, in more ways than one
16 Station that would air Bridgit Mendler and Demi Lovato hits
17 0–0, e.g.
18 ___ routing number (check info)
19 "What's the ___?"
20 @dril, by another name
21 TERF, e.g.
23 Pre-wedding errands
27 wikiHow subsection
28 Method of online scamming
30 Address after address
32 Like Nipsey Hussle's father
33 Site with gift ideas
37 Having a hard time letting go
39 Filter brand
40 Game makers, briefly
41 Can.'s smallest province
43 ___ Bub (celebrity cat)
44 Name on pasta sauces
45 Vending machine : food/drink :: ___ : dreams
50 Workers also called "disease detectives"
52 Pairs like oil and water
53 Fend (off)
54 Look after, informally
55 Approx.

DOWN

1 Common dressing
2 Hater, in fandom slang
3 Become too old for, with "of"
4 William McKinley High glee club member
5 Dreads
6 It might slow you down in Mario Kart
7 Go back and forth
8 "That outfit is fierce"
9 Visibly feeling something
10 ___ to go (eager)
11 Beginnings
12 Joke around
13 Is unable to continue
14 "What did I say?"
15 Animals that others keep evolving into
20 Risky time to bike
22 "Pagliacci" and others
23 Kept the IRS happy
24 Fisher of "Rango"
25 Like paper
26 Twelfth word in Hamlet's famous soliloquy
28 Something forward?
29 Onboard
31 A "hot" one might leak something
32 "Ta-da!"
34 Scrabble's has 100 pieces
35 Stuff for high steppers?
36 Youse guys's
37 Sellers of magazine space
38 "Short and stout" figure, in rhyme
39 Huge problem, slangily
41 Frequent flier?
42 Name that anagrams to a body part
45 Prefix for "wolf" or "rabbit"
46 "tb completely h ..."
47 Nurses
48 One of the Uto-Aztecan languages
49 Battle of ___
51 "Captain Underpants" author Pilkey

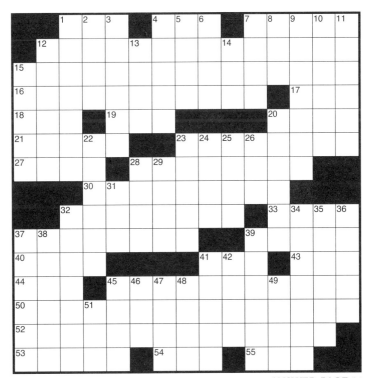

ANSWER, PAGE 84

ACROSS

1 Like WLW relationships
8 Astronomy units
15 Anthem whose French version uses the word "épée"
16 Cocktail recipe amount
17 Lady with paws, perhaps
18 Pygmalion sculpted her
19 What the "Í" in "Ísland" means
20 Cola garnish
22 Move recklessly
23 43-Across alternative
25 Come help?
27 Activity with a DM, briefly
28 Common root source
30 Company that often has to point out on social media that no, they are not putting oil on birds just so they can wash it off
31 Clips may hold them in place
32 Mauna ___
34 Not high on the rankings
36 Keyboard shortcut accompanying a "NO undo undo undo," often

38 Snitches
39 Textbook illustrations?
41 "Why are you standing?"
42 Policy ___
43 23-Across alternative
45 App category
49 Some addresses, for short
50 Third plotline in an episode
52 Ones (but not zeroes), e.g.
53 Pastry chef Dominique Ansel's "masterpiece," according to a 2013 Village Voice article
55 "Get off the stage" sounds
57 Senioritis may affect it: Abbr.

58 Add life to, as an outline
60 E-liquid container
62 It runs on Dunkin'
63 Large wardrobe
64 Like TMZ's most dedicated readers
65 Webkinz competitor

DOWN

1 Like people people
2 Tree that giraffes might snack on
3 It may be pending
4 Website logo format, often
5 Wave over, say
6 Elba who played Knuckles in "Sonic the Hedgehog 2"

7 Cooled (down)
8 It means "amazing!!" to Twitch gamers (and "wasn't that a '90s milk cap thing?" to most other people)
9 Large wrappers?
10 Pass along
11 Go at it
12 Grub hubs
13 Camouflaged Minecraft enemy
14 Classic Ford vehicles, slangily
21 Final, e.g.
24 "The clock app," formally
26 Wear the same clothes, say
29 Word replacing "word" in a math spinoff of Wordle

31 Mint sometimes used as a jokey name for 24-Down
33 Allies of autistic people, e.g.
35 ___ functions
36 Subjects of a gaming "war"
37 Zip
39 Go on talk shows, etc.
40 "Um, actually" type
42 Good speller?
44 Like a horse whose contents escaped at night, making it a horrible name for condoms
46 Bird thought to rank among the world's most intelligent creatures
47 Fortnite Competitive, e.g.
48 Ray-Ban offering
50 Either of the first married couple to win a Nobel Prize
51 "___ so busted!"
54 Seaweed snack
56 Sport lost by touching the ground with any body part that isn't the soles of the feet
59 ___ 20 (highest roll on a D20)
61 Cut (off)

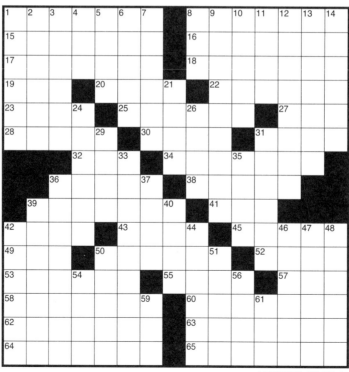

ANSWER, PAGE 84

23

ACROSS

1 Toy with cranks and wheels
6 Opens, as a bag of chips, maybe
13 Competitive Fortnite setting
14 One might tell you to "check engine"
16 When "Something wicked this way comes" is spoken, in "Macbeth"
17 Breakfast buffet feature
18 Toast meaning "To your health!"
19 Bygone Soviet space station
20 Ireland, to the Irish
21 Swashbuckler of the sky, in fantasy
25 "I'll be there," in texts
26 Dramatic "you can't know me"
27 Word that begins 23 California city names
28 "I touched the ___!" (schoolyard brag)
29 Struck gold
31 Valued for less, say
33 "Catch my drift?"
34 Catch
37 Harder to notice
40 Subjects of needledrop videos, briefly
41 Dungeons & Dragons, e.g.: Abbr.
44 Cadbury chocolates with gooey insides
46 In the style of
47 Agreement that may lower tariffs
48 Mendes of "Riverdale," to fans
50 The Bengals, on scoreboards
51 Try, as an aesthetic
54 Ball holder
57 Orphaned calf
58 Complete disarray
59 Write an impassioned Twitter thread, e.g.
60 Start of a historical recounting, maybe
61 Whiskey ___ (pub orders)

DOWN

1 Farm welcomes, from some
2 Sighting in Icelandic waters
3 "Schmoopy" and others
4 Begins
5 Moe's, e.g.
6 They're complied to without much thought, often
7 Seattle Kraken's org.
8 The Cavs, on scoreboards
9 Stripped down, as software
10 Some display pronouns above pics
11 Big ___
12 All over the place, with "about"
14 It might say "Your order is in the oven!"
15 Hacky end to a stand-up bit
22 Cribbage piece
23 "That's quite enough details about that"
24 Every one's partner?
26 Japanese for "dog"
30 Super cool
32 Something crawled through in spy movies
35 Defense
36 Letters for advice blogs, etc.?
38 "The ___ is on the floor"
39 Embarrassed
41 Approach quickly
42 Enjoy, as a swing set
43 One of two forming a zygote
45 Feign interest in
49 "Here's my thought ..."
52 Pub order
53 Hot Topic items
55 HBO ___ (bygone name for a Spanish-language channel)
56 Org. recognizing Alabama's achievements?

ANSWER, PAGE 84

24

ACROSS

1 Mutual support setup among YouTubers, casually
10 Site with lots of stickers
14 Condition for an Outlook scroller, maybe
16 Scandalous suffix
17 Gamers' "tennis rackets," maybe
18 ___ Winfrey ("Annoying Orange" character) (just kidding, but you bought it, right?)
19 Team effort in many offices
20 Someone who's gonna bust?
21 Dealer in futures?
22 Stringed instruments, for short
23 Provokes
25 Bygone M&M color
26 Rapper born in Gangnam, to nobody's surprise
27 Jane Lynch's role in "Glee"
28 Yet unseen
30 Safety cushion
33 Took a loss poorly
34 Still able to enjoy
37 Bender in "Futurama," e.g.
38 Tuque, by another name
39 Some delivery guys
41 "___ 2 Ü" (hyperpop track)
42 School announcement broadcasters
45 What one's mind can be
46 Certain hardwood tree
49 Sleeveless garment
50 Ivan the Terrible, e.g.
52 Word from the Hawaiian for "quick"
53 Around
54 Off your gourd, so to speak
55 Musical character who sings "Dear Connor Murphy / Yes, I also miss our talks"
57 Common software legal contract, for short
58 Much of "Hamilton"
59 Derive (from)
60 Browser information?

DOWN

1 Fixes, as a pocket hole
2 Inuit boats
3 British comedian Bill
4 Gets out of a position
5 Cheers at a bullfight
6 Male animal also called a "tup," apparently
7 "u can spell ___ as wrong as u want in the Gif tab n he still gon show up" (@whipaf tweet with an image of "sheogebuob" GIFs)
8 Remove from a post
9 Collection in a minifridge
10 Groups may be asked to check them at the door
11 Not have in the restaurant
12 Many a speedrunner
13 Longed (for)
15 Neckwear for the Eighth Doctor
23 Economic prefix for "zone"
24 ___ combined (winter sport)
27 Tender paid for a night out?
29 Good people-watching location
30 Particle measured in picometers
31 Something that does it well is timeless
32 Oppose
34 Dips quick
35 Speedrunner's bane
36 What thou art?
37 Sounds from piles of leaves
40 Likely more expensive
42 Historic name for Iran
43 Route that sounds agreeable?
44 Cars that inspired the production of Camaros and Firebirds, informally
47 They're hard to work with
48 Animal with striped legs
49 Quatre-___ (French stoner's favorite number?)
51 Wander
53 Makeshift "telephone" parts
56 Hotfoot it

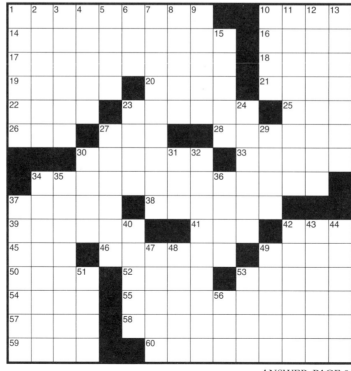

ANSWER, PAGE 84

25

ACROSS

1 Mango ___ (creamy drink)
6 Article in XXL Magazine, maybe?
9 Suffix for some online communities
12 Follow through with, as an urge
13 Family doctor, for one
16 Jeong's role in "Community"
17 Doesn't throw away
18 Visual ___ (Japanese aesthetic)
19 Keep away from
21 "Sounds good"
22 Start working for people
25 "This slide rules!"
26 Collection in a tower
27 Swiss coin
29 Getting dragged
32 Salon supply
35 "This disrespect is below me!"
38 They're flexed as a flex
39 Seek refuge in
40 Capable
41 "I'm a pirate!"
42 Elisha of elevators
43 Points from where someone's looking?
50 F⁻ or Cl⁻
51 Drinking buddies, e.g,
52 "If it's queer, it's here" app
54 National reptile of India
56 Over
58 Schadenfreude is a form of it
59 Harder to talk to
60 "The Impression That I Get" genre
61 Gets a name for, say
62 Some PCs

DOWN

1 Don't possess
2 Regretted that workout, say
3 They connect stories
4 "Cat's in the Cradle" character
5 Fortnite's V-Bucks, e.g.
6 Progressive Rashida
7 Like deities referred to as Devas and Devis
8 "Life of Pi" director Lee
9 Tiny hint
10 "I do" and others
11 They're difficult to comb through
13 Eliminate, in a certain Food Network show
14 "My opinion still stands"
15 Toonies, e.g.
20 Saturn ___ (apt anagram of "An SUV? True!")
23 "What? Of course not"
24 Boxy boat
27 ___-approved
28 Take a note from?
29 Place where many get lodged
30 Word that might cancel itself out
31 This many! (holds up a peace sign)
32 Shell station offering
33 Imitate a small dog
34 Ambulance worker: Abbr.
36 Many a resident of southeastern Turkey
37 Asgardian in the MCU
41 Disco-era suffix
42 Not new, quaintly
43 Has one's first glimpse of the morning
44 Permanent, maybe
45 Fruit ___ (mobile game)
46 Include as an inline email attachment
47 Tall tales
48 Coup target
49 Take great pleasure (in)
53 Onetime MTV VJ wannabes, likely
55 "Cheerleader" singer
57 When many periods took place: Abbr.

ANSWER, PAGE 85

26

ACROSS

1 Highest-grossing film until the release of "Star Wars"
5 Punny response to "What should I do with these cheese slices?"
9 Kinda
13 Surprised greeting
14 Unfinished software versions
16 Stick-y spot?
17 "You can look it up, it's true"
19 Adjective for some make-up palettes
20 Hard to see, say
21 Sushi eggs
22 Edward's mom in "Twilight"
23 First course of action
25 Road trip game
27 Bop
28 Go ___ (pull out all the stops)
29 Nintendo DS rival
32 Fetch
34 Nonbinary pair for some
38 It's hard to get past someone with these
40 Standing on the tippy-top of a ladder, e.g.
42 Ballet attire
43 Bygone jet, for short
44 [Nothing scheduled here yet]
45 Sound equivalent to "that's cold!"
46 Therefore
49 Distinguishing character
51 "I rule!"
53 School org.
54 "La Vie en Rose" singer
55 Not shut
56 Accompaniment for a dancer
60 Mitchell of "Teen Beach Movie"
61 Starts to melt, say
62 Prefix for "potent"
63 Windups
64 "Wow!"
65 KOA sight

DOWN

1 ___ down (note)
2 "That's soooo niiiice"
3 "Don't leave all this mess for ME"
4 Not run away from, as an emotion
5 Dot-com bubble success story
6 "For sure," in texts
7 Brand name that becomes an adjective when Q is appended to the beginning
8 Its current version is Sonoma
9 Source of some scars
10 That time I stood somewhat close to Björk at an airport, and others
11 Start of a concession speech?
12 Bird's sound
15 They're set by FitBit users
18 Closes securely
23 Letter representing the golden ratio
24 Not timely
26 Dejected comment after a disappointing gift reaction
30 Water-spraying playground fixture for small children
31 Locked account, in social media shorthand
33 Little pest
35 Word repeated into a mic, maybe
36 "___ get it now"
37 Xe/xem and 34-Across, e,g., for short
39 E-reader brand whose name anagrams to "book"
41 Lil ___ X
42 Inhabitant of a gift horse you SHOULD look in the mouth?
45 Result of phoning it in a bit
47 Complete turnaround
48 "Naturally, ___" (Canadian teen drama)
50 Pack of 78, typically
52 Things studied by period trackers?
54 Something tagged on Tumblr
57 Selection from a local brewery, maybe
58 First channel with 24-hour news coverage
59 Useful collection

ANSWER, PAGE 85

ACROSS

1 Slept some
14 Dessert made on a pan
16 Gorged on, as Oreos
18 ___ question
19 Solidify
20 Something to lean on
24 "Doonesbury" creator Trudeau
25 One of many in Pixar's "Cars"
28 "Diane Young" singer Koenig
29 Depiction on many a Christmas card
30 Three-syllable berry
32 Competitors in the World Cocktail Championship
37 "Flat" character of kids' books
39 Continued, as a storm
40 Many a trend starter, nowadays
42 Marlin's son in a Pixar film
43 Non-canon quartet?
44 Takes off, old-style
46 Not old-style
47 Publishing Triangle ___ for Trans and Gender-Variant Literature
50 Nicktoons character with two heads
52 "Avatar" world
54 Poked (around)
58 Scene set to "Eye of the Tiger," maybe
62 Friendly Internet greeting
63 Keith Haring and Shepard Fairey, e.g.

DOWN

1 Kinda gloomy, say
2 Repetitive learning style
3 Brewery collection
4 White, as vin
5 The ___ Times (era predating COVID)
6 Prefix for learning styles
7 ___ Pickles (youngest "Rugrats" character)
8 Sports injury site, briefly
9 PBS Kids Go! show that was hosted by Ruff Ruffman
10 Smart speaker device
11 Drying off, like SpongeBob after a shower
12 Meditation spot
13 More like a guru
15 "Can I haz ___?"
17 It'll create a buzz
21 Neighbors of Kyrgyz people
22 Stack at a diner
23 Focus, e.g.
25 Stick around
26 It may begin with a monologue
27 Anderson .___ of Silk Sonic
29 Hard to confront, maybe
31 Prohibit
33 Listing on a character bio
34 Apple site?
35 Its twin city is Paris
36 Depiction on many a Christmas card
38 Eye worker, likely
41 Disturbing ___ Peace (Ludacris label)
45 Shakespearean format satirized in Bo Burnham's "Words Words Words"
47 Just right
48 Say "Do NOT go in there" to, e.g.
49 Youngest sister in "The Amazing World of Gumball"
50 Boat at a cottage, say
51 2018 mobster film flop
53 Bris, e.g.
55 Goes
56 Acronym for an achievement shared by Rita Moreno, Mel Brooks, Whoopi Goldberg, and fewer than two dozen others
57 ___ ex machina
59 Pick up
60 Alana McLaughlin's sport, briefly
61 Not 'neath

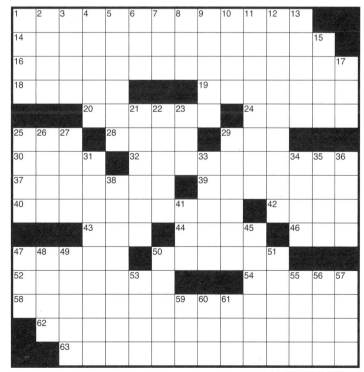

ANSWER, PAGE 85

28

ACROSS

1 Rorschach test feature
5 "<3" alternative, in sappy texts
8 Work extremely hard
13 Hot Italian hero?
16 Stretching effect
17 Showing up with expensive gear, perhaps
18 "Pain says you can't, ___ says you can" (commercial tagline)
19 City near Topanga State Park
21 Biting issue
22 ___-chef
23 Leaders of certain autocracies, historically
25 Her "Funny Girl" role would later be played by Rachel in "Glee" (and Lea in real life)
28 Talks too specifically about, as a show
30 Pre-transition label: Abbr.
31 Activity in a custom chair, perhaps
33 "Help me, ___-Wan Kenobi. You're my only hope"
36 Comedian with the hit Off-Broadway show "Get on Your Knees"
39 Word omitted from a "you up?" text
40 Classic Carroll character
41 Surrender
42 Rush (through)
44 Like soda garnishes, often
46 Word before "club" or "rock"
47 "Pinocchio" director Guillermo del ___
48 Self-help expert, say
49 Chinese entrée with seeds
55 Saunter
57 "How dare they!"
58 Sully
59 Outer layer of skin
60 "Hail ___"
61 Like dogs or foxes, apparently
62 Accidental coffee additive, maybe

DOWN

1 Partner 'til the end, briefly
2 Disney protagonist Pelekai
3 Processed mine samples
4 Cooking style with East, Central, West, and South varieties, briefly
5 Reading, writing, speaking, etc.
6 Impulses
7 Instrument that's one letter short of a another instrument
8 LGBTQ+-focused group on campus
9 Friend in early memories, say
10 Previews, as a link, maybe
11 Off
12 Shed old feathers
14 Not noticeable, as a stain
15 "What is DJ Khaled's favorite number? Eleven, because it has another ___"
20 Bud-dy film?
24 Communicate movingly?
25 ___ Blast (Mtn Dew flavor)
26 Jelly component, maybe
27 Holder of a McQueen-size mattress?
28 Strike, as a dragon
29 Needle source
32 Priv accounts, often
34 Soulquarians member Erykah
35 Mike and ___ (candies)
37 "You can't do that!"
38 The first O of Drake's OVO Sound
43 Looking-concerned?
45 Leader of K-pop's Red Velvet
46 "Looks good!"
47 Like many Sri Lankans
48 Cut
50 Nationality suffix
51 Soaks (up)
52 Webtoon whose titular character is the daughter of a ghostly spirit
53 Pursuit of Dr. Doom or Dr. Doofenshmirtz
54 JFL or SXSW, e.g.
56 Big stretch?

ANSWER, PAGE 85

29

ACROSS

1 Wait nearby for a response, say
6 Marker of progress, in some software
15 Follow, with "by"
16 Engineering branch that's not ... wait, maybe it is rocket science
17 "Ratched" star Paulson
18 Not close
19 MSG-rich food, casually
21 Toothpaste brand
22 ___entine's Day ("friendly" celebration)
23 Sprinted
24 Luna of "Sailor Moon," e.g.
25 Rolled up, as someone's windows?
27 Indistinct period of time, slangily
32 Birds in "O RLY?" memes
33 Country that's home to Tikal National Park
34 Brain freeze producer, maybe
35 Nerds, cutely
36 Round artifacts in photos
37 Pizza with your partner, e.g.
39 "Simpsons" character Krabappel
40 Big deals
41 Worry
42 Otherworldly beings, briefly
43 "Will pay later" letters
44 Abbr. in the title of video game score albums
47 Like unwelcome remarks, maybe
50 Many a sext
53 Tex-Mex staple
55 ___ Towers (longtime WWE headquarters)
56 "No need to be shy"
57 Use TurboTax, say
58 Avatars used by video essayists covering controversial topics, colloquially
59 Celebrated after a promotion, perhaps

DOWN

1 Invites to the penthouse, say
2 "Let me be clear" speaker
3 Embed in a Buzzfeed listicle, often
4 Cheese that's made backward?
5 Brings back on board
6 Purveyor of frosted tips
7 Abound (with)
8 Part of UAE
9 "Mazel ___!"
10 "Be gentle"
11 Crocs "setting" allowing for faster mobility
12 Brand whose hoodies zip up completely
13 Nails
14 Get for the day, maybe
20 "Don't do that, doggy"
24 Doesn't wait one's turn
26 "That sounds horrible, no thanks"
27 ___ Bees (balm brand)
28 Ontario by Ontario, e.g.
29 "Yer right, pardner!"
30 Jessica of "Fantastic Four"
31 Shout to a queen, maybe
32 Cuatro + cuatro
33 Animal in a viral remix of Taylor Swift's "Trouble"
34 "___ bin ein Berliner"
35 Attack in which a website is overwhelmed to the point of crashing: Abbr.
38 They'll prove if something's basic
39 Exploded in laughter
41 "Friend or ___?"
43 Wastes gas
45 Like old jokes
46 Dialed (down)
47 Get out of bed, e.g.
48 Nothing
49 Picture on a desktop
50 "Nah, Nietzsche"
51 Sephora competitor
52 Audiophile's collectible
54 "The Last of Us" network

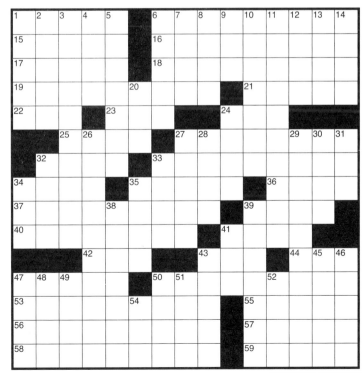

ANSWER, PAGE 86

ACROSS

1 Modified toy creature with an extended body
10 "Enough!" to an Italian
15 Any amount
16 Some saxophones
17 Plough : U.K. :: ___ : U.S.
18 Hard to get a reaction out of
19 Item thrown at a drag show
20 Like many salts
21 Comedian Byer of "Nailed It!"
22 "Come in," dramatically
24 Doesn't close
26 Made green, perhaps
27 Part of a drum kit
28 The Ove Glove, e.g.
29 2017 Margot Robbie film
31 Avoids buying, perhaps
32 "Yeah-huh!"
34 Icon in a Twitch chat
35 Nurse
36 Apple avatars
39 Chapek's predecessor (and successor) at Disney
40 Added muscle, with "up"
41 Finn the Human has very noodly ones
45 Simlish : "The Sims" :: ___ : "Despicable Me"
47 Fox role in "Teenage Mutant Ninja Turtles"
48 Display of soup cans, maybe
49 Coffee dispensers or ash jars (look at that range!)
51 "Mask up" ad, e.g.
52 Something extra
53 Most credible
55 When some footballs are hiked
56 Pong, e.g.
57 "Watership Down" director Martin ___
58 Blows up

DOWN

1 Hit over one's tennis opponent's head
2 Like ogres, according to Shrek's simile
3 Say "you are NOT valid"
4 Mars, but not Earth
5 Laurence, in "Romeo and Juliet"
6 They call the strikes
7 Persuades to join
8 Like pants
9 "Quit ___ joshin'!"
10 Foundation
11 Non-traditional stand-up, e.g.
12 Sinking to a new low, say
13 Eau de ___
14 Attempts at conquering Mount Everest, e.g.
21 WSJ competitor
23 Pronoun in brand tweets
25 Org. dealing with a lot of breakdowns
27 "Yoo-___!"
30 Whole bunch
31 Bollywood star Kapoor
32 Delivery alternative, in pizza ads
33 Some barbecues
34 Word after "beach" or "dad"
35 Be utterly devoted to, in slang
36 "I've done stuff I ain't proud of. And the stuff I'm proud of is disgusting" speaker
37 Connected, as a bathroom
38 Mob animal
40 Whoa, this is blowing up!
42 Say again
43 "I'm baaaaaack!"
44 Introductions at auditions
46 Shrink-resistant synthetic fiber
47 "80's Ladies" singer K.T. ___
50 Emperor whose bust has a wack hairline tbh
53 SpongeBob, to Mr. Krabs
54 Swiatek of tennis

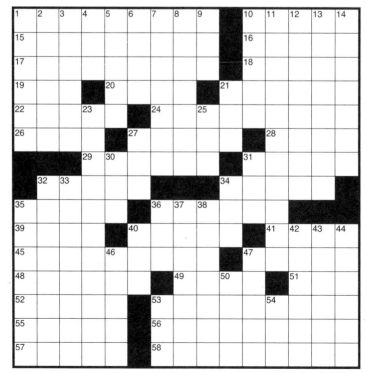

ANSWER, PAGE 86

31

ACROSS

1 Escort through the door
7 Laundry cycle
14 "Is that a problem?"
15 Celebrate, in a way
16 Damascus resident
17 Not cranked up all the way
18 Twenty-four
20 Org. with a style manual
21 Fencer's point
24 Stereotypical hacker's comment
25 Crunch, e.g., notably
26 Gets into a crash
29 Farm newborn
30 E-learning center
33 First places for many
36 Discount that's not offered on the website, e.g.
38 "What does he do, this man you ___?": Hannibal Lecter
40 Greatly desires
41 Dispensary purchases
42 "This is the ___ you're dying on?"
44 Playwright Soyinka
45 Proposed economic model, for short
46 Large estate, in Spanish
49 Twitter alternative
51 Where pets get purrfectly pampered
55 Helping stay (up)
56 The McDonald's logo, e.g.
57 Transitions from day to night
58 Greece's capital

DOWN

1 Part of macOS: Abbr.
2 "Watch it!"
3 Bass Pro Shops item
4 Provincial flowers of Quebec, before 1999
5 "It happened in front of me"
6 Bad idea
7 ___ scheme (investment scam)
8 "Top" dish
9 Ideal place
10 "ABC gum" remnant
11 "The Muppets Mayhem" drummer
12 Do some body-building?
13 Bodybuilder, e.g.
15 Consuming dread?
19 Cutting and shaping kit
21 Prefix for "tourism"
22 Home for koi
23 ___ Decor (magazine)
25 Freebie at Home Depot
27 Difficult to erase
28 Software makers, briefly
29 Repurpose without permission
31 Zelda's land
32 Valuable containers?
34 Badass, briefly
35 ___ bean (tiny creature)
37 Gravity Falls's state: Abbr.
38 Company with Crosstreks
39 Tesla's opponent in an Epic Rap Battle
41 Sends down the list, at an open mic
42 Lost all patience
43 Desktop images
46 Optimist's trait
47 School sports org.
48 Have the zoomies
50 Covers in Cottonelle, e.g.
52 "___-Hulk: Attorney at Law"
53 Tool for writing 27-Down
54 ___-backward

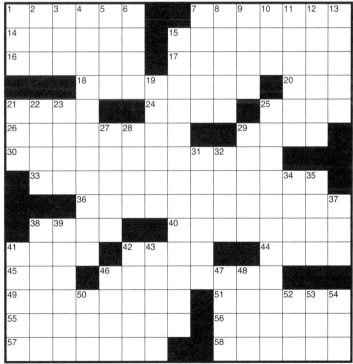

ANSWER, PAGE 86

ACROSS

1 "Zootopia" popsicle-pusher
6 Did laps, maybe
10 Queens airport code
13 Spanish "ma'am"
14 Rings sometimes served with chili sauce
16 Friend of Pooh and Roo
17 Common capacity for a French press
18 Pointers
19 B, to A
20 K-Cup : Keurig :: ___ : Tassimo
21 Rcf. it's much easier to let the library be in charge of owning
22 "Yu-Gi-Oh!" villain
23 Establish your turf?
24 Brandon ___-Mohammed (Canadian comedian whose name includes two "Pokémon" trainers)
26 Nailed
27 Inseparable pair on "Community"
32 #Deep social media post that led to the spin-off meme "SBEVE"
33 Demi, e.g.
34 Forehead protuberance
35 Course for budding bilinguals, briefly
36 Respected individuals, briefly
39 Book whose world you're already immersed in?
41 Most-viewed body part, I would suppose
43 "Stop saying that about me!"
45 Caked over
47 Not trained, say
48 Add a parenthetical to, e.g.
49 Coffee brand with a Baked Apple Pie flavor
50 Has a laugh
51 Popular Garageband preset
52 ___ day
53 It's not a big house, but it's a twig house
54 Put in stitches

DOWN

1 Oddball
2 2017 title character for Aubrey Plaza
3 Designs that increasingly seem to feature sans-serif text and nothing else
4 "Whose Line Is It Anyway?" host before Aisha Tyler
5 What I shove my Q-tips in because I live in the REAL WORLD
6 Coffee go-with, for some
7 Didn't wax?
8 Newell of "Glee"
9 European archipelago
10 Like some pie crusts
11 Gave a warm reception
12 Easily lost audio accessory
13 Hockey card info
15 Identify incorrectly
21 "AHA"
25 Buckwheat noodle
27 Greek god from which a Marvel villain's name derives
28 Historically unhoppy beverage
29 Cancelled
30 ___ ex machina
31 Skiers call it an "avy"
32 Setting for Colombo
33 2014 Chadwick Boseman film
34 Breaks from adulting, say
36 At first?
37 Drove around on a cart for most of the day and then hit some balls a few times
38 Herd member
40 Start to get registered
41 ___ position (padmasana)
42 Not trained, say
44 Blu or Jewel in "Rio," e.g.
46 4/20, e.g.
47 Diamond figures

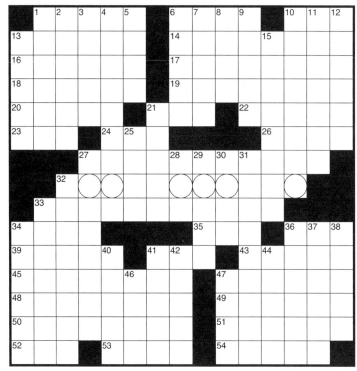

ANSWER, PAGE 86

33

ACROSS

1 Label in some transition before-and-after posts
7 Simmer down
14 More squarish
15 "... I'm listening"
16 Horse ___ (low karate position)
17 Dip with zip
18 "There's no reason for me to be here anymore"
20 Failure
21 Adobe Illustrator feature for creating paths
22 Producer of "Op-Docs," for short
23 Like the Jackbox Games mascot
25 Puts to work
27 Popular merch items
28 "___ Been Thinking About You a Lot Lately" (Onion headline)
31 Muralist Diego
33 Marmalade-making tool, maybe
34 Not in the dark about
36 Chucked
38 People overstaying their welcome at a party, probably
39 You might try to get them to turn pro
40 "The Sweetest Taboo" singer
42 Ruby alternative, to coders
43 Living authentically, in a sense
44 Awkward interview pause, e.g.
47 Monthly midway point
49 SpongeBob SquarePants's "Dammit!"
51 Puzzle where the numbers in a grid's rows and columns determine which boxes are shaded
53 High
55 Like Twitch streamers, usually
56 Stolen vehicle
57 Eyes
58 Map features

DOWN

1 "Viewers Like You" network
2 Atta bread!
3 Requirement for an Urban Dictionary submission
4 Ones looking for long-term relationships, maybe
5 Scout's job, briefly
6 University in Peterborough, Ontario
7 "Black Panther" director Ryan
8 "I'm ___ you!"
9 Extra NHL periods
10 Bandmate of Niall, Harry, Louis, and Zayn at one point
11 Urban Dictionary, e.g.
12 Impossible kid to feed
13 Dines like royalty
15 ___ theory
19 Anemone, to name one
23 "Elvis" director Luhrmann
24 "Can I speak?"
26 JoJo of "Dance Moms"
27 People who are up for trying things out?
29 Linked up with
30 God who's an anagram of his half-sister Ersa
32 Hi-___ vest
35 Hooting bird
37 Duchamp's "Fountain," e.g.
38 Embrace, with "into"
39 Like some car washes
41 Prefix for some skin products
45 Miso base
46 Indulge, as an impulse
48 Rise dramatically
49 La ___ Tar Pits
50 Behind
52 Some baseball execs
54 They often give referrals: Abbr.

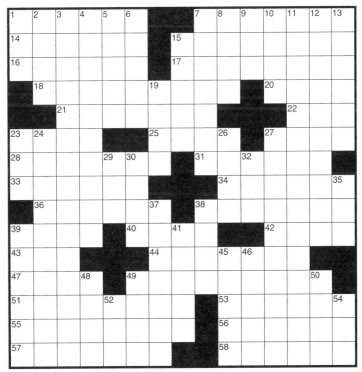

ANSWER, PAGE 87

ACROSS

1 Have no date
7 Stuck on
14 Human study course, briefly ... or a prefix for a yearly furry con
15 Strong hold
16 Most minimalist
17 Psych-out, e.g.
18 Very
19 It may precede a blessing
21 High school diploma alternative, for short
22 Was crushing on
24 Sites for C-sections
25 One pouring red after the kid's in bed, maybe
26 "As a result ..."
28 Texting abbr.
29 Audible
33 Split, as a coconut
34 The Who and The The, e.g.
35 Nickname for Philosophy Tube founder Thorn, which drops the "gail"
38 Prefix for "save" or "tune"
39 Made, as a case
41 Terrible
42 Some eye accessories
46 Capital near Provo, Utah, briefly
47 Customizable labels on subreddit posts
48 French seasoning
49 "Watch your language"
51 Egyptian god of fertility
54 Laughing stock?
55 Needing attention RIGHT THIS SECOND
56 Providers of reaction shots?
57 App where I keep swiping right on ads :/

DOWN

1 Talk nonstop
2 For the hell of it
3 Kush and Diesel Haze, e.g.
4 First word of the "Addams Family" theme song
5 "___ Poetica"
6 Smonked some wonk
7 Deep sadness
8 Ball on the court?
9 "Down where it's wetter" (darling, it's better, take it from me)
10 Default user pic on Twitter, once
11 Prolong
12 People giving you the light at the open mic, e.g.
13 Newspaper opinion pieces
15 Said "hey hello" on AOL, maybe
20 Like the lion slain by Hercules
22 Certain content labels, briefly
23 Drink that used to bring people to their knees?
27 Boo <3
30 Letters between monikers
31 One-piece outfit
32 R-e-a-l-l-y clarifies
33 ___ a thousand (reach perfection)
34 Actor whose iconic quotes include "Do you think God stays in heaven because He too lives in fear of what He's created?" and "How do you do, fellow kids?"
35 Stuck
36 Way to be direct!
37 Passports, for example
38 Unable to respond, say
40 Give, as tasks
41 "I have your answers!"
43 Brown of "Cutthroat Kitchen"
44 Blue mineral in Minecraft, familiarly
45 Put a name to?
50 Liveliness
52 ___ Lanka
53 "69," as opposed to int(69), in Python: Abbr.

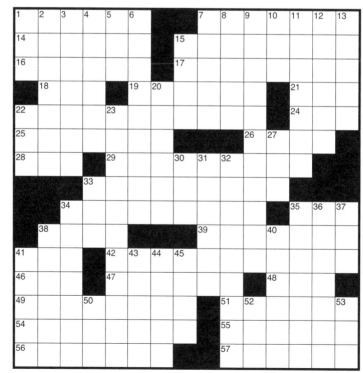

ANSWER, PAGE 87

35

ACROSS

1 "My package!"
7 Common deliverer of packages
10 "Stop stalling"
13 Triangular letters
14 Natural order, in East Asian philosophy
15 Frequent Lennon collaborator
16 Helen Parr, familiarly
18 "The Best Day ___" ("SpongeBob" song)
19 Wong of "Tuca & Bertie"
20 Ghostly goo
22 Dinar spender
24 Visit
25 Visibility concern, for short
26 Wi-Fi necessity
28 Give notice to, say
31 Vigilante's goal, maybe
34 Trucker's motto?
37 Follow-up to a much-liked post
38 Enjoys
39 Uncomfortable direction to look, for many
42 Long Beach–based school, briefly
43 Cool thing to ride like a scooter at the grocery store
45 "Despacito" artist Fonsi
47 Gay punk offshoot
50 Meditation advocate ___ Chinmoy
51 bit.ly and linktr.ee, for two
52 Like some jeans
56 Syst. for actor CJ Jones
57 Part of the L.A. Kings?
58 Draw
59 Affirmation to a queen
60 Trans activist Johnstone
61 Super Smash Bros. actions

DOWN

1 Seeds, in a sense
2 Advance handler
3 "Sofia" artist
4 Address symbols
5 Dojo padding
6 Author Edugyan
7 ___, New York (supervocalic city)
8 Word before "animal" or "bus"
9 By one's lonesome
10 Rule against Juuls
11 Digits that end about 25% of prime numbers
12 "Would you still love me if I was a ___?" (question in a meme)
17 Suffer epic pwnage
18 2023 Pixar film with the tag line "Opposites React"
21 Default Mac software
23 Tapping-on requirements, often
24 Welcomed
27 Like the transfer window for some transit cards
28 "Be saved!"
29 IHOP ___ (pancake delivery service)
30 Place for a wall-mounted basketball hoop, perhaps
32 Palindromic holiday
33 Made to think differently
34 Defeated in the ring, briefly
35 Record label hidden in "demisexual"
36 Ova
40 Act like a fool?
41 Nonstop, as a flight
43 ___ butter
44 Come up
46 12 on a pair of dice, e.g.
47 Waterfront sight
48 "Bear" in constellation names
49 Body part clinged onto by a toddler, for many parents
53 Freshly painted
54 Commentator Navarro
55 Name that becomes a rude acronym with an F inserted

ANSWER, PAGE 87

36

ACROSS

1 Youth identifier at a concert, often
10 Type of weave
15 Simp for, say
16 New York city name-dropped in the "steamed hams" scene, in "The Simpsons"
17 Private discussion
18 Arrangements of dirty clothes
19 Bugs, e.g.
20 Buddy's transportation to New York in "Elf"
21 Timor-___ (Asian country)
22 Subject of the song "Let It Grow" in "The Lorax"
24 Animals that, aptly enough, get narrower at one end (just go with me on this one)
26 Departure
29 Drinks like a cat
31 It's the place to go!
32 Tire problem
34 Phillipa of "Hamilton"
35 Kesha's "TiK ___"
37 Someone conceived on Halloween will likely be one
38 Always product
40 Like pseudoscientific claims
43 Eponymous physicist André-Marie
45 ___ de Cristo Mountains
46 Dress/perform like Kitty Scott-Claus
47 Music lover's thrift shop find, maybe
49 Subject in telenovelas
50 Unclosed tabs, e.g.
52 End of a celebration?
55 Letters with labels
56 Popular component of 1950s salad recipes, for whatever reason
57 Know-it-alls
59 ___ wrench
60 Bodies that seem to "almost be hitting Earth" every year, like ugh, we get it, you're scary, can you leave us alone
61 Low-affect
62 Text dump?

DOWN

1 Crisp home theater purchases
2 "Can you forgive me?"
3 Joking around
4 Rae in Olive Brinker comics, e.g.
5 ___ serif
6 NPR merch item
7 Focus on something different?
8 Event that prompts many fashion review videos
9 ___-transition
10 Play extender?
11 Up for debate
12 Turn, as a phone
13 Company with slush funds?
14 Lil ___ X ("That's What I Want" rapper)
21 Try to decipher, as a Zoom participant on mute
23 Improv legend Close
25 Shovel's sister, on "Blue's Clues"
27 Impossible to change
28 Comedic foils
30 Nintendo character without much depth?
33 Self-appointed office party role, maybe
36 Many a resident of Turkey/Iraq/Iran/Syria
39 Long-running Canadian teen drama franchise
41 Knickknacks
42 Quarantine, briefly
44 Making out on the Jumbotron, e.g.
48 Bolognese alternative
50 XPS producer
51 "Enchanted" role in a 2004 film
53 Ooze
54 Set to zero, as a scale
56 Poke
57 Single with the most-searched lyrics on Google in 2020
58 Suffix for "rom" or "zom"

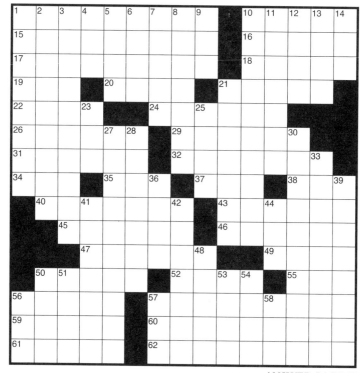

ANSWER, PAGE 87

37

ACROSS

1 "Numb Little ___" (Em Beihold hit)
4 2022 film about a smart speaker
8 Castle protectors
13 One working out a bit, maybe
16 Sleep issue
17 "Carry on, then"
18 Gone, as cookies from the cookie jar
19 Experimental space
20 Buildup in Patrick Star's belly button
21 Puts out
22 Restaurant called "PFK" in Quebec
25 ABC show with Zee, briefly
26 Muse's instrument
27 Start scheming
30 Spy kit accessory
33 Love and kindess, it's said
34 Bro
35 Mufflers
36 Wiener ___ (something blown in an orchestra)
40 Locale for a Donald Glover sitcom, briefly
41 "Yo ___ ..." (palindromic introduction)
42 Activity with meeples
44 "Can't Stop the Music" number featuring diving, wrestling, etc.
46 Animal Crossing character
48 Nooch, e.g.
50 Like partners in crime, maybe
51 Leonhard credited with popularizing the use of π to represent 3.1415...
52 2000s teens who wore skinny jeans and colorful clothing and dyed their hair, probably
53 Spread out
54 Read, as a text
55 Get riled (up)

DOWN

1 Lodging on the water
2 Ask me what this is :)
3 Spring from the Icelandic for "one who gushes"
4 Some fuzzy fruits
5 Rapper who debuted with "Rhyme Pays"
6 Insignificant
7 >:(feeling
8 "Feel Good" comedian Martin
9 Libra stone
10 Vaccines, e.g.
11 Publication following Disney Channel stars, maybe
12 ___ lap
14 "Our Lady of Paris"
15 It's hard to avoid
22 Bursts with pride
23 Unhinged
24 Sorceress who changed Odysseus's men into swine
27 Tonsil ___ (making out)
28 Nickelback drummer Daniel
29 "
31 Perfect settings
32 Telecom company whose logo contains ten vertical lines (include the letter I)
33 Time when the teacher expects a present from you?
34 Line accompanying an eyes emoji, maybe
35 "Don't deny me this!"
37 Boston's Central Artery/Tunnel Project, more familiarly
38 One of the founding nations of the Iroquois Confederacy
39 Means of ___
42 Close on set
43 "Wake Me Up" singer Blacc
45 Far from land
46 Shortcoming
47 ___ fixe
49 "Do or do not, none of this ___ crap": Yoda after losing all patience
50 .xml alternative

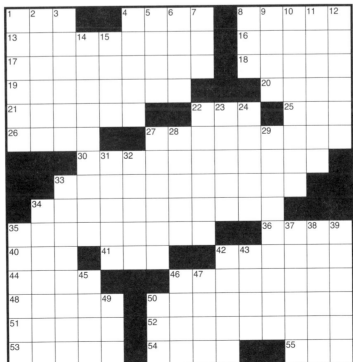

ANSWER, PAGE 88

38

ACROSS

1 Wicked
8 Some basic sandwiches
15 Coming through a speaker
16 Lurker's spot
17 People with takes
18 Play that's the first recorded instance of the idiom "wearing one's heart on one's sleeve"
19 "Who ___ this happen?"
20 Blew up
22 A dot or a spot, but a large one it's not
23 Using as a bed, say
25 Apt snacks to serve at a crossword tournament
26 Like the gender identity kathoey
27 Fa'a ___ (traditional way of life on a Polynesian island)
29 Hostile org. in "The Simpsons Movie"
30 Make physical, in a way
31 Blows, maybe
33 Wrist injury
35 "A man has fallen into the river in Lego ___" (ad catchphrase in a meme)
37 In "A Quiet Place," those who make it don't make it
38 Powerful women, in slang
40 Lose momentum
44 "That's amazing!"
46 E-girl emoticon
48 Jacket style
49 Subheader in the online travel guide WikiVoyage's entry for "Sleep"
50 Common birth control method
52 Her heart will go on
53 Lin's best friend, in Duolingo lessons
54 Enter like you own the place
56 Regular: Abbr.
57 Some make-up collections
59 CW show about a morgue assistant who eats on the job
61 Vibe
62 They squeak in apartments
63 Transfem pronoun pair, sometimes
64 Disparity observed in labs, e.g.

DOWN

1 Course for the college-oriented, briefly
2 Bug on the phone
3 Paragon
4 "Great ___!" (after-show compliment)
5 Mama ___ ("Princess and the Frog" character who sings "Dig a Little Deeper")
6 Small opening?
7 Guarantee
8 Album holder of a sort
9 Word in many snack food names
10 Condition whose intersection with autism is represented by adding a "u" after the first letter
11 "f.k.a." alternative, perhaps
12 Creature that might "tail-walk"
13 Calendar used before the Gregorian
14 "I'm BLUSHING"
21 Livens (up)
24 Protections from the rain
26 Nickname for "Diners, Drive-Ins, and Dives"
28 "See ya, Léa!"
30 Song of praise
32 Instruments for the plucky?: Abbr.
34 Play observer
36 "I don't wanna spoil it"
38 Transmission part?
39 Hit (at)
41 Phrase accompanying outstretched arms
42 Peak literature?
43 Have roots
44 Gravy ingredient
45 "Can we meet at like ___? I'll be finished with lunch by then"
47 Opens, as a jacket
50 With 55-Down, update regarding a bug fix, e.g.
51 "Carmen" composer
54 Gets over a breakup faster, jokingly
55 See 50-Down
58 Feature of the teacher's edition of a textbook
60 "This tastes so good"

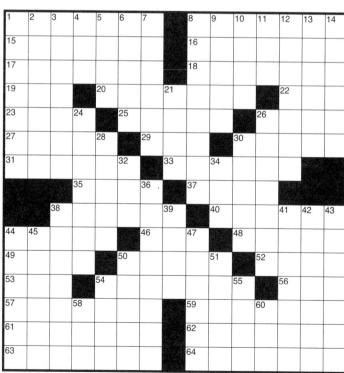

ANSWER, PAGE 88

39

ACROSS

1 Batman's butler
7 Vaccine-endorsing org.
10 Rae of "Barbie"
14 "The last name is a coincidence"
16 Jewel believed to be from the Sanskrit for "jewel"
17 Site for international posts
18 Name on Clamato packaging
19 Collection
20 Uncomfortably moist
21 Objects pondered upon
22 One may convey daggers
23 Teensy
24 Crouches for safety
27 ___ of Wikipedia (Twitter account highlighting odd Wikipedia screenshots)
30 Prefix with "therapy"
31 Where ointment may be applied
32 TV's Cory Matthews, notably
35 It encompasses MCU's Phase One, Two, and Three
38 TikTok post, e.g.
39 Des Moines demonym
40 Edmonton hockey player
41 "Duh!"
43 Like some processed wheat
44 Producer of oom-pahs
45 Museum trips?
47 Video game series that often features songs re-recorded to match its world's language, with "The"
48 Adjective on news sites
50 Network that broadcast both "Schitt's Creek" and "The Kids in the Hall"
53 Place to gyre and gimble, in a poem
54 Lead-in to a fact check
56 One of the Twelve Olympians
57 Segue into an important life lesson, say
58 Where YouTube video essayist Sophie, Ziggy Stardust's Spiders, and men (per John Gray) are all from
59 Ambient music pioneer
60 "But despite all that ..."

DOWN

1 "___ Marching" (Dave Matthews Band hit)
2 Information on a fantasy wiki
3 Word before "bro" or "house"
4 Energize, with "up"
5 Synthesizer-heavy genre
6 Part of the Texas Triangle
7 Like terrible-quality video, jokingly
8 Gloom's partner
9 Upset, in baby-speak
10 Insect with spotted wings
11 Sarcastic "Go team!"
12 Waited patiently
13 Burners, briefly
15 Type of ski lift
22 Prefix with "permanent"
23 "Make a move"
24 Surveillance system on screens, briefly
25 Greeting to an unexpected visitor
26 Nickname for "420"
28 Ellie Kemper role on "The Office"
29 Show affection toward, maybe
31 "Bop!" singer JoJo
33 Arch type that sounds like a sarcastic remark
34 Location in Kelis's "Milkshake"
36 "Who is this ___?"
37 Fine sand
42 Stan, with "over"
43 Enjoys some oolong, say
44 Ornament also called a diadem
46 They might poke out of a muscle shirt
47 Tried some different strokes
48 Sport similar to skeleton
49 "Damn right!"
50 Be overly sweet
51 Color of Bandit Heeler, in a children's show
52 Focus of many "Dr. Pimple Popper" episodes
55 Help

ANSWER, PAGE 88

ACROSS

1 Closes with a click
10 Tattoo artist's supply
14 Ontario-based women's hockey team from 2020 to 2023
16 "___ use this chair?" (start of a confusing audition monologue, on "Mr. Show")
17 "Stop calling me 'that guy'!"
19 ___ boss
20 Seeing something?
21 The tiniest bit
22 Lead-in to a texting aside
23 Notable feature of Schnozmo, on "The Fairly OddParents"
24 Romans, in Rome
27 Nickname applied to misidentified driftwood, often
31 #1 spot?
33 ___ for nerds (YouTube video data, by its official name)
34 Jazz guitarist Montgomery

35 Umbrella term that includes bi and pan: Abbr.
37 "Chill on the details"
38 Creators of negative buzz?
41 Sweetie
44 Genre with moody beats
46 "Elena of Avalor" setting
47 Dunker's dunk-ee
49 Accessibility option for the hearing-impaired, briefly
50 Isabella Garcia-___ ("Phineas and Ferb" character)
53 Set to come in
54 Playful bite
57 Disney channel show conflict, often

60 "That makes sense ..."
61 Problem in the middle of a stream, perhaps
62 "___, your fly's down"
63 Flirty emoji

DOWN

1 Wave one's hands around, e.g.
2 NYC neighborhood near NYU
3 ___ League
4 TikTok posting with dramatic acting, often
5 Star-bellied (or not) character in a Dr. Seuss story
6 Bundle up
7 Refine, as one's craft

8 Country where pencil crayons are called "colored pencils": Abbr.
9 Pumbaa's pal
10 Most gag-inducing
11 Prefix for 22-Down
12 Get all up in a bunch
13 "Dancing With the Stars" runner-up JoJo
15 Gas in flash lamps
18 Words of agreement
22 One failing a Turing test, I'd hope
24 Prop for Wonder Woman cosplay
25 "It's their ___"
26 Absorb, as yolk with bread

28 Composer Erik
29 "Relatable"
30 Giller Prize–winning novelist Edugyan
31 React to a compliment, maybe
32 Prefix for "fauna"
34 Gabbi Tuft's former org.
36 Mathematical study of continuous change
39 Visionary
40 South Asian wraps
42 Zoomed past
43 Some work machines, briefly
45 Spoiled pug in Disney's "Pocahontas"
48 "NICE, I hadn't thought of that!"
50 ___ of Theseus (thought experiment)
51 [I'm a bad kitty!]
52 Matures
53 They may be connected through detective work
54 2019 role for Beyoncé
55 Big Apple?
56 Dog-eared thing, at times
58 "Hon hon, why yes"
59 Frequent caller?

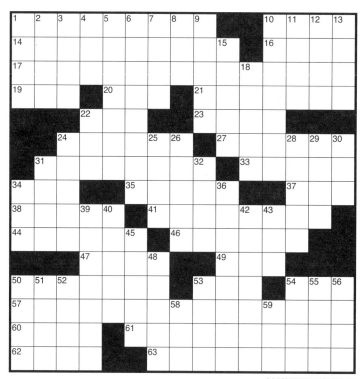

ANSWER, PAGE 88

41

ACROSS

1 Rap's Kid ___
5 "You guessed too high"
9 Place for a party, in a Weird Al parody
12 "Aren't you forgetting something?"
13 Bring to mind
15 Warped Tour sponsor
16 Male 1-Downs
17 Suffix with "dacno," for the compulsive urge to bite people
18 Spiral paths?
19 Classic diner offering
22 Scary ___ (pioneering Irish rap group)
23 Erotica often explores them
24 Some have toe clips
27 "___ Lot" (Stephen King novel)
28 Caught a whiff of
29 Org. that becomes a school when its first and last letters are swapped
32 Place for a 1-Down, maybe
33 Ambience for a study session, maybe
37 Sole singer on BTS's "Epiphany"
38 Like saying "do you live for your OWN SELF, or for your CELL-PHONE?" (damn)
39 It might end on a high note
40 Goofster
42 Comedian on the road, e.g.
43 Disrespects
45 Word by a paper airplane icon
46 Title for a fictional character with enby vibes, in memes
50 To whom Sarah McLachlan says "I do believe I failed you," in a 1997 song
51 Slice on a pickle platter
52 Boast after the big game, maybe
54 "Robot ___" ("Phineas and Ferb" song that begins "It's gonna be a mechanized melee / A bit of a big bot brawl")
55 "I'm ___ here"
56 Lymph ___
57 Peter on peanut butter
58 End opposite the face, on some hammers
59 Attack

DOWN

1 Pet going "prrrr" or "prrp!"
2 Mistake, cutely
3 An "-itis" is named after a musician's tendency to get attached to one
4 "Expect your meme to appear on my own social media"
5 King Julien and others
6 Not answer, as a question
7 Part of ESC, in European TV
8 Enjoyed Alta, say
9 Tapping machine
10 Its official language was Quechua
11 Look over, as damages
14 Shows mercy, in a sense
15 Jell-O product
20 Smut
21 Place for a party, in a Miley Cyrus hit
24 Acronym for a Starbucks offering that's pretty gourd?
25 Reference with a "Smileys & People" category
26 It's corny to start an important speech with one
29 Harambe, e.g.
30 Comedian Michael
31 Cut (off)
34 "Sounds about right"
35 Sports broadcaster Arledge
36 It'll help move your canoe
40 E flat equivalent
41 Give purpose, maybe
42 Capital whose website has a .ir domain
44 Refill
45 Puerto Rico might be one, eventually
47 Celebration
48 Wolf's cry
49 "Goo-goo or goo-goo not, there is no ga-ga" (Baby ___ quote, I'm guessing)
53 Pickleball partition

ANSWER, PAGE 89

42

ACROSS

1 Check at the door, maybe
5 Zoroastrian priests
9 Reason one might take Motrin: Abbr.
12 Radar prompter, maybe
14 Singer Myra Ellen better known as Tori
15 Prominent ___ch feature
16 Songs like the version of "WAP" where Cardi B says "wet and gushy"
18 Love of "Ned's Declassified School Survival Guide"
19 Typically
20 Absorb
21 Isolated, say
22 Depiction in "Big Bang Theory" bumpers
23 Posted on Twitter, jokingly
24 "Dear diary, today sucked," e.g.
26 Talked back to
27 They may be recited with a pounding fist
32 Non-binary bio phrase, for some
33 Not allowed inside, maybe
34 Dips (out)
35 Dr. Drakken's sidekick in "Kim Possible"
39 "Burnt" Crayola shade
40 "Immediately!"
44 Financial field, for short
45 Restrains
46 Clothing spots
48 Roth ___ (401k alternatives)
49 Fruity dahi drink
50 Number of enneagram types
51 Basic math calculation
52 Exhausted or wasted
53 Tags
54 Relinquish control of
55 McKinnon of "The Big Gay Sketch Show"

DOWN

1 First word in a Megan Thee Stallion parody where the word "savage" is replaced by "Baskin"
2 Support program for drinkers' families
3 Biter unwelcome in the kitchen
4 2021 Olivia Rodrigo hit
5 Unhappy with
6 Hermano de otra madre
7 "Ha. Pranked."
8 Orbiter whose emblem depicts 15 flags: Abbr.
9 Asks for a hand?
10 Records that may have a list of motions
11 Lobbed unhelpful comments
13 ___ socks
15 Phosphoresces
17 Major division
20 Busts, maybe
25 Foes of restaurateurs, maybe
26 Maple taffy ingredient
28 Canva and PicsArt, for two
29 Lakshmi by another name
30 Bae
31 "Brokeback Mountain" director Lee
32 Horses well-adapted to desert climates
33 Star removal from the Good Noodle Board, e.g.
34 Royal Canin competitor
36 Search engine that uses its ad revenue to plant trees
37 Prepared
38 Type of gridiron kick
40 Trunk content, maybe
41 Muscular
42 Many unicellular organisms
43 Ring declaration: Abbr.
47 Sitcom alien seen on "Young Sheldon" and "Mr. Robot"
49 "___ and Me" (heavily sponsored 1988 flop)

ANSWER, PAGE 89

43

ACROSS

1 Beach Boys hit
7 Field units
12 Land, as a big fish
13 Like your monitor, hopefully, after you give a thumbs-up gesture
15 Chillin'
16 Music in an IG story, often
18 Will Shortz's paper: Abbr.
19 "Mamma ___!"
21 "I've made out with a caveman," e.g.
22 Pass it!
24 Ackerman in "Attack on Titans," e.g.
26 Ora on the "Fifty Shades Freed" soundtrack
27 "No time to talk!"
28 Cultural ___
29 Pop trend?
30 Nissan offering
31 Event where you can see eye-to-eye with your higher-ups?
33 What some fanbases call themselves
34 Text response to an inside joke
35 Signal that you've finished the exam, maybe
36 Arts workshop
37 Bring on, as a high schooler to cook burgers
38 "No ___ Allowed" ("SpongeBob" episode)
39 "Ghosted" star de Armas
40 Angry Birds enemy
41 LMFAO member?
42 ___ ring (bit of body jewelry)
45 Moved like a Rock 'Em Sock 'Em Robot
48 Grow fond of
50 Brunei has one
51 "Don't feel too bad"
52 Boy band with JustiN, ChriS, JoeY, originally JasoN but he was replaced by Lance who was nicknamed LansteN for commitment to the bit, and JC
53 Says

DOWN

1 ___ Academy (online education resource)
2 Like many cereals
3 "Heart-Shaped Box" songwriter Cobain
4 "Bravo!"
5 Like socks you grabbed without looking, perhaps
6 Walking quietly
7 ___ Toy Barn ("Toy Story 2" setting)
8 "Gangsta's Paradise" rapper
9 Encounter
10 Desirable brownie section
11 Être : French :: ___ : Spanish
14 Record collector?
17 Indulge
20 Pong company
23 Dish sometimes served with kecap manis
24 Lean component
25 Tool for online alcohol retailers
26 Makes easier to identify, as a file
27 Emissions that can pass between atoms
28 Slides into EVERYBODY'S inbox
29 Taking off like a shot
30 Like editorial decisions
31 Beyoncé alter ego
32 Animal for whom the first and last letter of its name combine aptly
36 Sea with 150+ islands
38 Able to improvise, say
40 Buddies
42 Strauss known for riveting material
43 Thing
44 Some coffee containers
46 "GET OUT OF THERE"
47 Quadrennial event with a blue color scheme: Abbr.
49 WNBA player Nurse

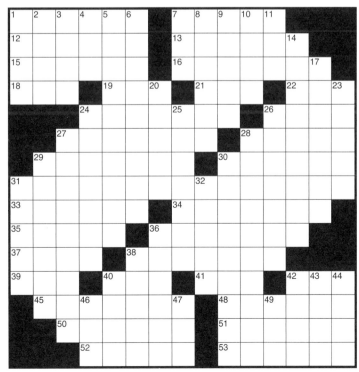

ANSWER, PAGE 89

44

ACROSS

1 Dish that should not be served to an unsavory individual?
10 Flower shop collection
15 Discord server overseer
16 Cutesy-wutesy text to a partner
17 Sun's classification for its first 500,000 years
18 Words said when walking in, taking one look, and walking right back out
19 Toronto's Yonge and Dundas, e.g.: Abbr.
20 Descriptor for some color names
21 Footballer nicknamed "O Rei"
22 Eerie feeling, sometimes
23 Not trans
24 Mens ___ (guilty mind)
27 Not over DMs, e.g.
28 Lead-in to a harsh truth
30 "This suuuux"
31 Mitch Hedberg and others
35 Limited edition 2023 Nabisco cookie with a meta flavor
36 Famous rebuke to Joe McCarthy

37 Vader's nickname as a kid
38 King Charles III, e.g.
39 Sends a notification to, say
40 "Huh!?," online
41 "My pet rat is missing!"
42 ___ Original (rice brand)
44 POM product
46 Get on the ground
47 Show from which Elvis Costello was banned for over a decade: Abbr.
50 Package prepped for up-and-leaving
52 Game with "quantum" and "ultimate" versions

54 Something scrubbed away
55 Number determining chess matchups
56 Winter driving hazard
57 Their rooms aren't roomy

DOWN

1 They'll call you out
2 "Madagascar" mouse lemur
3 "Estoy ___ velas" (Spanish phrase meaning "I'm broke" that literally translates to "I'm on two candles")
4 Bumped into
5 Steel, e.g.
6 Art ___ (annual Swiss fair)

7 Constantinople resident
8 Audibly give up, maybe
9 [These Canadian winters are rough!]
10 Predecessors of TikToks
11 Nowhere to be seen
12 They take on large legal battles
13 Word repeated after "New Year's," on December 30th
14 Looking guilty, as a crewmate
21 Sign of the "true Lord of the Dance," per Weird Al's "Your Horoscope for Today"
22 Notable feature of 35-Across

23 Vegan alternative to a breakfast staple
25 Roast host
26 "While I'm talking about it ..."
27 A part of life, say
29 Téa of "Bad Boys"
31 Hawaiian word for "family"
32 ___ Cup (trophy that went to the Toronto Six in 2023)
33 Be audibly amazed
34 Defensive trenches
35 Become less icy
41 Number considered lucky in Chinese culture
43 One of seventy in this grid
45 Part of a contractor's quote
46 Reinhart of "Riverdale"
47 Stop masking one's autism, say
48 Bar ___
49 Tour segments
50 Many taken lesbians, for short
51 Word after "CBD" or "THC"
52 Vietnamese festival
53 Silicon Valley higher-up, briefly

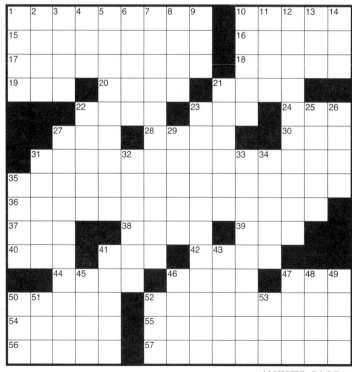

ANSWER, PAGE 89

50

45

ACROSS

1 Series finales, often
11 "Sesame Street" character ___ Cadabby
15 How are you making out?
16 There for the taking, say
17 How Twitch streams unfold
18 Bunny voiced by Kristen Wiig on "The Looney Tunes Show"
19 Squirrel (away)
20 Lavish attention (on)
21 "Wonderwall" band
22 Garment with a pom-pom
23 Island in some dirty limericks
25 "Gadzooks!"
27 Look after Mittens, say
28 Poison ___
29 Resonant sound accompanying the THX logo
31 Come up, as a need
33 Descriptor for credit in "WAP"
34 Fiber-rich cereal ingredient
35 "I ___ thought of that"

37 Corpus Christi and others
41 Part of BPM or MPH
42 Prepares, as cheese for nachos
44 Hatcher of "Desperate Housewives"
45 Literally, "nourishing mother"
47 Function whose wave crosses the point (0,0), for short
48 Effect in some hydraulic press videos
49 Soccer star Mia
51 ___ the lore (fully in the know)
52 Assistant told to "pause Apple Music," e.g.

53 "Let's get you out of the cold"
55 Lifehacks may highlight unconventional ones
56 "I feel you!"
57 Profs' necessities
58 Satire website with a "Woman-spiration" section

DOWN

1 Like some Snyder's products
2 Old, euphemistically
3 "Papaoutai" singer whose name is an anagram of "maestro"
4 "That was a close one"

5 Letter descended from the Phoenician letter heth
6 Like ghosting
7 Perform a Gregorian chant, say
8 Cause a disturbance
9 Units in a flashlight
10 Catch, as an easter egg
11 Company whose name is quacked in commercials
12 Close guy friends
13 "Can you ___ this?"
14 Like a sourdough starter
21 Deliver better bars than
24 Royal headwear

26 Cross-shaped control on a GameBoy, for short
27 Vampire Weekend album with "California English"
30 Label on some "all-natural" foods
32 Playing extra for a winner, for short
34 Log of grog
35 Extremely unpleasant
36 Having a protective layer
37 Like some dumplings
38 Period of rest
39 Tubes in old tubes
40 Saints' counterparts
41 Refuse
43 Not going anywhere?
46 "Something's ___" ("I'm getting weird vibes")
50 [This category could contain anything]: Abbr.
51 Group dissolved on Dec. 26, 1991
53 Focus on the road, say?
54 It's picked by the picky

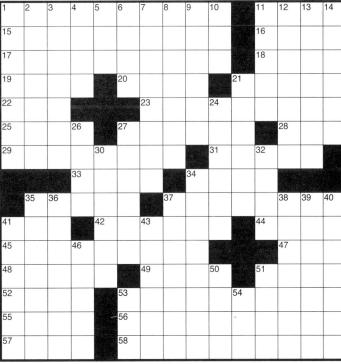

ANSWER, PAGE 90

46

ACROSS

1 Barbs that may cut deeply
14 Mindset focused on neither loving nor hating your appearance
15 "Crowd should be good now. Break a leg!"
16 Word on a green drink bottle
17 Points out
18 They're far out!
19 Chicken strips, cutely
21 Digitally produced, as a Transformer, e.g.
23 They're gained in football: Abbr.
24 Enlists
26 It has pages, but no paper
29 Thyme amount
30 Relax after a busy shift, maybe
32 Hikaru ___ ("Star Trek" character)
33 Its spokesgecko's name is Martin, apparently
34 Dr Pepper Cherry, e.g.
35 Holland of the MCU
36 Heracles overcame its lion, in Greek mythology
37 Something inserted into a 34-Across
38 "Why, you're right!"
40 ___ tai
41 Thing to be conscious of?
42 22-Down's action
46 Many a family-owned supermarket
47 Not worth talking about, maybe
48 Second largest of the Hawaiian islands
49 Some holistic professionals
54 Subjects of the website Fold'NFly
55 John Cena's "The Time Is Now" and others

DOWN

1 Element at the upper left of the p-block
2 "Let's talk in private," on Twitter
3 Sheridan of "Ready Player One"
4 Crosswords not published in mainstream outlets, slangily
5 Can't go without
6 Doesn't use teeth
7 "Rugrats" dad ___ Pickles
8 A minor one might give you the E-B-G-Bs
9 Having fun on stream?
10 Works after hours, maybe
11 "___ on the G String" (piece sampled in Red Velvet's "Feel My Rhythm")
12 Room with a clothes chair, maybe
13 "Lady Marmalade" singer
14 Hay bundle
15 Angkor ___
20 "beats me"
21 Around
22 What gives?
24 Some plants
25 Nothing at all
26 Childish suffix for "best"
27 Marker of beach limits
28 Mexico's first major civilization
29 They're in it for the long haul?
31 Part of a fursuit
33 Bronzes on the beach
34 Activity done with a fidget toy, maybe
36 ___ Falls (Ontario or New York city)
37 Try to suss out, as words on a Mad Gab card
39 Green ghost in "Ghostbusters"
40 "Thank you for the lei"
42 Antagonists in copaganda, often
43 Smoothly transitions (into)
44 Bonkers
45 "Correct, my formal chum"
47 Adjective for mortals or flesh wounds
49 Imitate
50 Bolted
51 ___-in (not required)
52 Sunny D alternative
53 Like someone represented by a blue, yellow, and pink flag

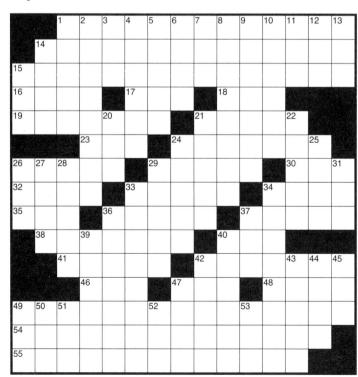

ANSWER, PAGE 90

52

47

ACROSS

1 Support
7 Acer products
10 Engrave
14 One with whom you might share a "chore chart"
15 Tackle in an Onion article, say
17 Set of unknown length, in mathematics
18 Sam Ryder song with the lyric "I've searched around the universe / Been down some black holes"
19 It's the end of the world as we know it, but they feel fine
20 Raced (through)
21 Triage sites, for short
22 Fooled
23 Fooled
25 Adjective for a cool "cat"
26 Spitters
29 Gender-neutral possessive
31 Comment after a post-dinner watch check, maybe
36 Character who calls Remy "Little Chef," in "Ratatouille"
37 "What song is this?" response, in memes inspired by its ubiquity in gaming videos
38 Not following
39 ___ Moines, Iowa
40 Wyo.'s neighbor
41 Some foods serve as "replacements" for them
44 Hypotheticals
45 Space to relax
47 Most August births
49 It's "Not Unix!," in a recursive acronym
50 Source of the smiley face in "¯_(ツ)_/¯"
52 "Skrrt!" and others
56 Design for a Touch, e.g.
57 Ball in "Castaway"
58 Ultimate Guitar offerings
59 "What a shame"
60 Digital wallet company

DOWN

1 Coffee ___
2 Coffee ___
3 Wilson of "American Vandal"
4 It may result in a fine, for some equipment
5 Something made o' fish, on a McDonald's menu
6 Be overrun (with)
7 ["Look over here!"]
8 Some guitar equipment
9 What some paintings seem to do
10 Afore
11 Causes for historical division?
12 Card ___ (Cards Against Humanity role)
13 Coop matriarchs
16 Utensil that could also be used for 28-Down in a pinch
22 Complete the first step
24 With disrespect
25 Label on many shawarma menus
26 Setting
27 Inspirations for "want-repreneurs," briefly
28 Leaves for lunch?
30 Keyboardist with an "Arkestra"
31 Consumed
32 Presentations that might go viral
33 Fork point
34 Yes-___ (adds to, as an improv suggestion)
35 Titular island resident in a 2008 film
42 Puts out without permission, say
43 Barack's choice to replace David
44 Kolkata's country
45 Presentation at an assembly, say
46 "___, Can You Hear Me?" ("Yentl" song)
48 Smooth out
49 Look slack-jawed
51 Classified listings
53 Canada's Rogers, e.g.: Abbr.
54 Feathery drag accessory
55 Show from which some rejected sketches were used on "I Think You Should Leave," for short

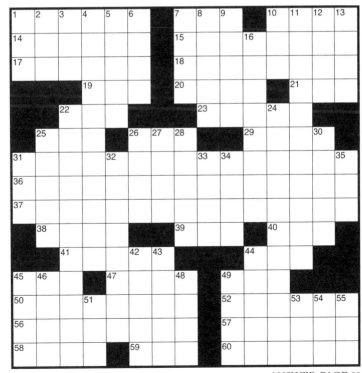

ANSWER, PAGE 90

53

48

ACROSS

1 Country folk?
10 Character often shouted at by viewers
14 "Hold on, I got a joke too ..."
16 Cenozoic and others
17 Like some scratch-off tickets
18 Hype playlist contents
19 Private eyes, in old slang
20 Popular tabletop roleplaying game, briefly
21 Fish transportation method, in a 2019 meme
22 Hold out for
24 Sesenta ÷ diez
26 Driver on set, sometimes?
27 Rapper who once tweeted "gonna start back releasing music soon the old town road money running out"
30 Like Manny in "Ice Age"
32 4G ___
33 Home of Texas's Eiffel Tower
36 Food Network personalities
37 "So the guy responded ..."
39 It has blades that cut blades
42 Insensitive response to "your always so mean to me"
43 Award for the NBA's Nikola Jokić or Joel Embiid
46 "You got the joke, right?"
48 Damage to it may cause tinnitus
50 Second and fifth word of a popular poem template
51 Cartoon nemesis of Perry, for short
54 Feel
55 Pull up, as a webpage
57 Ice cream cone feature, maybe
60 Not know from ___
61 Titular character in a 2016 stop-motion film
62 "I'm fully who I am" speaker, on a Time magazine cover
64 Helper in a film lab?
65 Firmly established
66 "Creep" singer's first name
67 Focus of many Julia Kaye comics

DOWN

1 Have many talents
2 "TOLD YA"
3 Black coffee is 5 on it
4 Gives a pass, maybe?
5 "How We Do (Party)" singer Rita
6 Fix, as a relationship
7 "Resident Alien" nurse ___ Twelvetrees
8 Ontario's Orangeville and Oakville, e.g.
9 Insinuating
10 Prevalent theme in "Squid Game"
11 Beto who I bet-o could land a kickflip
12 Bar fight?
13 Bread heels, e.g., humorously
15 "Dump! Them!"
23 Like chopsticks
25 "I knew they'd fall for that"
28 John Kramer's franchise
29 "Xylophone" alternative, in alphabet books
31 ___ : Zooey Deschanel :: Him : M. Ward
34 Looking for, on dating apps
35 Swivel on an axis
37 "That's kinda funny"
38 Glass on the radio
39 HelloFresh delivery
40 "Oooof"
41 Anime body pillow owner, maybe
43 Official order
44 Facial expressions
45 Doctors-in-training, briefly
47 Drenched
49 Give generously, as praise
52 Baby with a flat face
53 Manicurist or tax worker, in different senses
56 College hangout spot, typically
58 Kelly of daytime TV
59 Abandoned, in poetry
63 How-___ (tutorials)

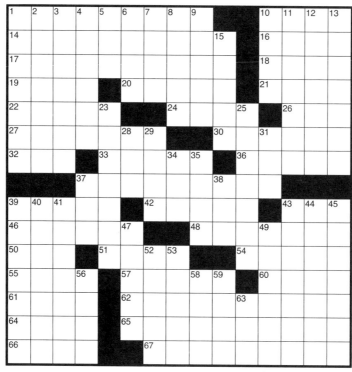

ANSWER, PAGE 90

49

ACROSS

1 Soaked
7 Abe, to Bart
13 Jetson who the Internet decided was born in 2022
14 Floor-cleaning robots
15 Rank that rhymes with "Henson"
16 [rimshot]
17 Within walking distance, say
19 Space Invaders company hidden backwards in "negotiate"
20 Chuck roast cut
21 Submitted
22 Desire
23 Best friends 4 ___
25 Sumac whose name reverses to another name
26 "Feel free to reach out"
31 Stays in a savings account, say
34 Sinking in an office chair?
35 "¿Que ___?" ("What up?")
36 "Seven Year Itch" artist James
37 "___ bonne heure!" ("Splendid!," in French)
40 Doesn't pay, as fare
43 Transport bought in response to rising gas prices, maybe
47 Some babies have two
48 Handful of aces?
49 Brand that killed its mascot Mr. Peanut in 2020 for some reason (don't even get me started on Baby Nut)
51 "Hey Arnold!" character Helga ___
52 Response to "Just write a number, any number" in a "Celebrity Jeopardy!" skit from "SNL"
53 Baby's outfit
54 "Apparently!"
55 When they go off, they're on

DOWN

1 The OWCA in "Phineas and Ferb," for example
2 Lady of Poe poems
3 Going over the head of
4 Court orders
5 Waffles that may be Thick & Fluffy or Grab & Go Liège-Style
6 Guy who might end on a high note
7 Intensifier before "yes" or "no"
8 Way to go!
9 Jordan's capital
10 ISTP or ENFJ, e.g.
11 Chilling pursuits?
12 Like "alas" and "alack"
14 Palindromic .zip alternative
16 Some teenage entrepreneurs
18 Take place?
21 Its products are slept on
24 Cumberbatch's Cumberbitches, e.g.
26 "___ Harris Goes to Paris" (2022 film)
27 "___-huh!" (eloquent counter-response to "Nuh-uh")
28 Fakes out, in hockey
29 One traveling through an "elver pass"
30 Floridian airport code
31 Tries
32 Auli'i of "Moana"
33 Rings for a table?
37 Relaxed
38 Come through the ceiling, say
39 Risk playing pieces
41 Great ___ (big dogs)
42 Lauder with a cute accent … sorry, I mean an ACUTE accent
44 Guitar accessories
45 Muscat resident
46 Animal whose name is etymologically related to the word "water"
48 Nickname that anagrams to a color
50 Anticipatory night

ANSWER, PAGE 91

50

ACROSS
1 HelloFresh package
4 "A snack, ___ given as a reward or inducement" (start of the OED's definition of "Scooby Snack")
7 Common bacon flavor
12 Bible figure that anagrams to a body part
14 Sactown's state
15 Not giving off an "I love going to parties" vibe, say
16 Reaction to a cute GIF from a partner, maybe
17 Lots (of)
18 Piano-playing dog on "The Muppet Show"
19 Subreddit for sharing progress on HRT
22 Device that'll warm your buns
23 "Wow, we're pretty much the same person!"
24 Nuzzling in the mall, e.g.: Abbr.
25 Choose, with "for"
28 Freeway entrance
31 Duo with the albums "Party Rock" (2009) and "Sorry for Party Rocking" (2011)
33 "Yucky!!!"
36 Quiet points
38 "Assuming that's the case ..."
39 One going to heaven for SURE
41 Tiny dots
43 Basic first-aid technique
44 Province with MiWay and Züm transit systems: Abbr.
46 "Say It (To My Face)" band Meet Me @ the ___
49 The NBA co-founded one for NBA 2K in 2017
54 "Blame It on September" boy band
55 Like some thrills or talk
56 What a housecat is in their mind's eye, maybe
57 Problems on set, maybe
58 Must
59 Regarding, on a memo
60 Sensible
61 Video game sprite, e.g.
62 See 7-Down
63 Seasonal Starbucks quaff, in posts

DOWN
1 "Community" cast member David
2 "Hey, what's up, you guys!!" and the like
3 Bob the ___ ("VeggieTales" character)
4 Wipe out
5 Pop-up video effect?
6 Ananas in "Téléfrançais!" is one
7 With 62-Across, euphemism for "sex toy"
8 Enjoying one's own company
9 Shut down
10 Reacts to a meme, maybe
11 Part of 31-Across (the acronym, not what it stands for)
13 Lower with a dumbwaiter
14 Lady with pointed ears, say
20 "The wait will be short"
21 Drug that VR can elicit the effects of
26 "Je ne parle ___ français"
27 "I know the feeling all ___ well"
29 Where "Bluey" is from
30 Brony's fav franchise, briefly
32 Confuses (for)
33 "Argh, I forget the shortcut for how to exit full screen" button
34 Cardi B/Megan Thee Stallion hit
35 ___ access point (something 34-Down can stand for)
37 Like the Bermuda Triangle
40 Palindromic position
42 Alaskan ___ Kai (dog breed)
45 26-Down, in English
47 "Licorice Pizza" discourse topic
48 Long sentences
50 Schedule
51 Rapso performer
52 "The Princess Bride" prop
53 Vehicle about which Henry Ford's son probably felt some kinda way when it flopped, since it was named after him
54 Satisfying discoveries
55 One of the three root words for most translations of "tea"

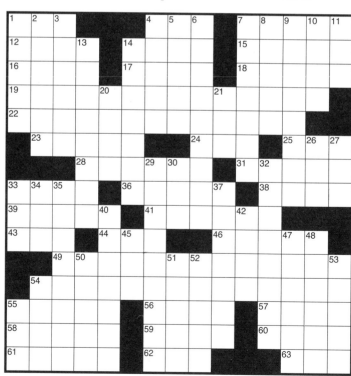

ANSWER, PAGE 91

51

ACROSS

1 Lust after
10 Shout out, say
15 Ate for eight?
16 Cravalho of 2024's "Mean Girls"
17 Bearing someone's letters?
18 Its first letter stands for "treasury"
19 "___ the point I was trying to make ..."
20 Going stat?
21 Man cave ... for her
23 Gets on the ground
25 ___ Buddy (drinking-based social media app)
26 Not prone to crushing, briefly
27 "You look adorable!!"
28 See 5-Down
31 Leaves the country, maybe
33 MGM founder
35 When most light leaves the sky
36 Word before "cheese" or "industry"
39 "Krazy" craft supply
40 Relays, as information
41 Foodie
43 Put on a scale
44 French Mrs.
47 Stuff in the bowl but not the scoops, on cereal boxes
48 Filipino pork dish
50 Their "Max" variety is over-ear
52 Way to go?: Abbr.
53 Xfinity, e.g.
55 "___ them!"
56 Lo-fi albums, often
59 Disingenuous commenter
60 Fibrous leftover in the kitchen
61 Puts into boxes
62 Consumes while steaming, perhaps?

DOWN

1 Oreo variety
2 Capital whose name translates to "sheltered harbor"
3 Posing as
4 Link ___ (feature of "decaying" old websites)
5 Looked with 28-Across
6 "... huh!?"
7 Make a crane, e.g.
8 Undesirable body count for a stand-up show audience
9 Indian Ocean inlet
10 Bases for some poutines
11 Some USB devices
12 Greeting in 2-Down
13 One + tree + fife, to a pilot
14 "That's where you're wrong, ___"
22 Stand-up comic's greeting before going on to make ten minutes of jokes about rain, perhaps
24 Frightening item for a trypanophobe
25 Feel certain
27 Diamond positions: Abbr.
29 "Tunak Tunak ___" (viral Indi-pop hit)
30 Straight, casually
32 Callaloo containers
34 Spicy snack morsel
36 The Batmobile, e.g.
37 Deteriorate
38 Opposite of WSW
40 Burger of the Day feature, on "Bob's Burgers"
42 "Rock the ___" (1982 hit by the Clash)
44 Tall posts
45 Prefix for "managing"
46 Result of trying to divide by zero, usually
49 Try to stop
51 Throw hard, as snowballs
52 Totally invested
54 Seasonal Starbucks quaffs, for short
57 Org. that's a reversal of 58-Down
58 Animal that's a reversal of 57-Down

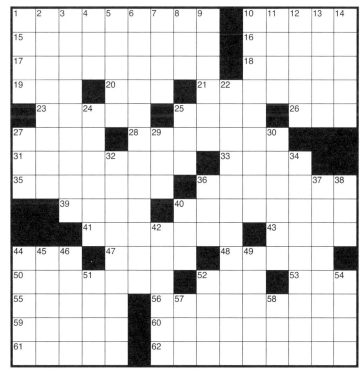

ANSWER, PAGE 91

52

ACROSS

1 Candace's stepbrother, in a Disney series
5 Very large, humorously
11 Google Chrome alternative
13 Likely to assume someone has a hidden agenda
14 Beginning of many online community names
16 How arguments may be deployed
17 "Really?"
19 Stated
20 Guided tour of a museum, say
22 Googleability concern, for short
23 Feature of the Beanie Baby named Crunch
24 Securing, as a gate
28 "Get ___ here!"
31 Avoid an obstacle on the right, maybe
32 Follow-up to "We don't have Coke ..."
34 "Got an extra controller?"
36 Money for Cubans
40 Many trolls who engage in the bad-faith "hey, I'm just asking questions" type of online dialogue called "sealioning," slangily
42 TikTok, e.g.
43 Org. whose job is taxing?
44 Where flights to Queens land
47 First step
49 Fizz-ical business location?
50 Something rolled out in a P.E. class, maybe
52 "Already?"
55 Butlers, e.g.
56 Type of question answered with a thumbs-up, maybe
57 Anxious
58 Mull (over)

DOWN

1 Supporting
2 4-track releases, e.g.?
3 Depending (on)
4 Staple of ska punk
5 ___ Dance (TikTok's parent company)
6 Suffix for "serpent"
7 Bombay Sapphire products
8 Pretend that
9 Most important
10 Cunning type
12 How garage sale items are sold
13 Activity in flexible relationships?
15 URL letters
16 Where many march out and about?
18 Sites with scenic photos in their post previews, probably
20 Brass installed to keep the books in order?: Abbr.
21 Lucy of "Kill Bill"
25 "... ___ quit!"
26 Hoof sound
27 Palmer of "Nope"
29 One of the Belchers on "Bob's Burgers"
30 "Have ___" ("Don't just stand there")
33 Face masks, gloves, etc.: Abbr.
34 Particular
35 Deem to be beyond criticism
37 Tweet out during a tough time, slangily
38 Nail polish brand
39 Business that aptly rhymes with "ahhh"
40 El ___ ("Suicide Squad" character)
41 Figure (out)
45 Word in a cookie brand name
46 Tomatoes : bad performance :: ___ : good performance
48 Ran, as ink
49 Sensical, as an argument
51 Canada : dart :: U.S. : ___
53 Ace value, sometimes
54 "... and don't wait to do it"

ANSWER, PAGE 91

53

ACROSS

1 Sci-fi villain who sings "Daisy Bell"
4 Part of a pirate ship
8 Ultra- alternative
12 Prefix with "angle"
13 Like many bodybuilders
14 The sandwich's supposed namesake et al.
16 Content of some British pies
18 Go over with a pencil
19 Madonna Thunder Hawk's people
20 "Jennifer's Body" actress, 2009
22 Squeezes (by)
23 Name that reverses to a fruit
24 ___ redistribution (effect of HRT)
25 Slangy initialism meaning "bravado"
26 Feng ___
28 Drink with a cherry blossom on the can

36 Video with six-second memes
37 Performers asking for suggestions
38 Bread cooked on a tawa
39 Helene D. Gayle and others: Abbr.
40 Compensated sick days, etc., for short
42 Chills
45 Something made for a microwave dinner
47 Muss, as feathers
49 Digging in a garden
52 Influencer with winged eyeliner, often
53 Did an Italian run, e.g.

55 Diet that eschews grains and dairy, for short
56 Narwhal's home
57 Checking org.
58 They may be graphic
59 Icelandic dairy product
60 Where "oink" might mean "honey, I'm home!"

DOWN

1 Visual editor alternative, often
2 Opera solo
3 It may need to be activated for an Internet connection at the office
4 Papas' partners, in 1960s folk-rock

5 The A in LGBTQIA+, briefly
6 Give a stern talking-to, say
7 Depiction on a pole
8 Mastodon enjoyer, e.g.
9 Make, as money
10 People who spray it when they say it?
11 Brand of foil
13 Hand (out)
15 Get spicy in the DMs
17 Diet soda originally marketed towards men
21 Model Bündchen
25 Hat part that some bend
27 More like a 60-Across

28 Twitter profile pic, for short
29 Cactus relatives
30 New hobbyist
31 "Breaking Bad" network
32 Mail-sorting center, briefly
33 Thing avoided by swishes
34 Forever (ago)
35 The A of Q&A: Abbr.
40 Set up a full week of meals, e.g.
41 ___ the heartstrings
43 Bills in un portefeuille
44 Dust particle
45 "___ Madness" (long-running murder mystery play set in a hair salon)
46 Verb at a bank or library
48 Like the best things in life, it's said
50 Make a treehouse?
51 Greeting with an apostrophe
54 "Get back here!"

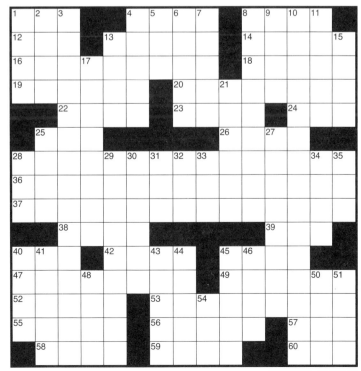

ANSWER, PAGE 92

54

ACROSS

1 Had a steady look (at)
6 Clinton's group, briefly
11 Expert
14 Cheesy autobiography subtitle
15 He's a real fixer-upper!
17 Word after "pig" or "dog"
18 How a reversible jacket can't be worn?
19 Vehicle with an unexpectedly large capacity
21 "Will of the People" rock band
22 Unlike public accounts
23 More grainy?
24 Property claim holder
25 ___ of chaos (menaces)
27 Grab
28 Food mentioned in Weird Al's parody of "La Bamba"
31 Left figure, briefly
32 Location where people cut and wrap
33 It'll disrupt a flow
36 Typical weekend length
37 Establishment with cats, sometimes
38 Baseballer Suzuki
40 Out, maybe
42 Item included with many an IKEA purchase
43 Clothing company known for using untreated denim
46 ___ Cat (early Internet meme)
47 Training facility filled with pushy people?
48 "It's hotter in here than usual"
50 Samba o merengue, por ejemplo
53 Doesn't have a good vibe
54 Style, fancily
55 Way out there
56 Ballet bends
57 Zoom alternative

DOWN

1 "She was a big-boned ___ from southern Alberta ..." (start of a k.d. lang lyric)
2 Like from the menu?
3 It covers all the spots
4 Doing taxing work online?
5 "From the beginning," a bit pompously
6 Put on paper
7 Manmade border
8 Word for the act of raising children?
9 Shaving alternative
10 Joke
11 Add up (to)
12 Charities' concerns
13 Emulate Sandman or the Wu-Tang
16 "People Puzzler" host Leah
20 Brave soul
22 Car freshener scent
23 Puppet material
24 Trip planner's need?
26 Turns rotten
29 Al Pacino character in a 2021 crime drama
30 "Moon Person" statuette, for short
32 "imo" alternative
33 Like some cellphone plans
34 Not many
35 Part of MLM, in dating contexts
36 Maple Leafs' org.
37 Take a limo, perhaps?
38 Hard-to-traverse waters
39 Copernicus on the Moon, e.g.
41 Breaks down
42 Check for freshness
44 ___ signals
45 Best Play and others
47 Piece of set dressing on "Our Flag Means Death"
49 Supernatural ability
51 Shock
52 Was full of beans?

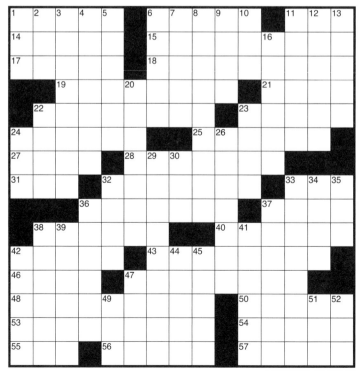

ANSWER, PAGE 92

55

ACROSS

1 "Stay in your lane, bub"
8 Digs
13 Supported a neighborhood bistro, e.g.
15 ___ floor
16 Works with lines like "Carmen, you just trippin', 'cause you know I love you infinite"
18 Playground retort
19 Muscles that sound like the first word of 24-Across
20 They might be taken around the block
22 Hit back?
24 Hopes to get
26 Burst of wind
29 Sounds heard in a hedge?
30 Note for the unnoted?
31 They're unlikely to pass
33 Some hitchhiking stops
34 "Truthfully ..."
37 Call on
38 Used, cutely
39 Subject of a "torn" ado?
40 They want to meet leaders, stereotypically
41 "And others," in papers
42 Trademarked THX sound
45 FOR ___ NAVIDAD (punny sign vandalism)
49 Put one and one together?
52 Crossword framework
53 Surname descended from the Irish "O'Maolgaoithe"
54 Celebrated after touching down, maybe?
56 Less "up"
57 Like scabs
58 Revival agreements
59 Tidies (up)

DOWN

1 ___ and all
2 Breakout console
3 Not hot, as a crowd
4 Nailbiter
5 2011 film about a drumming bunny
6 Tracy Marrow, familiarly
7 Compensation for a container
8 Absolutely delivers on, as a verse
9 Vinegar and others
10 Brought new meaning to
11 Relatives of the Renaissance instrument the dulcian
12 ___-cone
14 Like the (wildly unuseful) word ZZZ, in the Scrabble Dictionary
17 Opposite of "ease"
21 Follow-up to a corny line
23 Color-changing fixture in some smart home devices
25 Inexperience after a break, slangily
27 Used for the night
28 Was attracted to, with "for"
31 Like some "Chew"
32 Binary digit
33 Like having the word "elegant" in this clue, per crossword conventions
34 ___ kid (tech-obsessed toddler)
35 [D'oh!]
36 Zero, e.g.
40 Joins
43 Lick one's paws, e.g.
44 "The Office" receptionist
46 Schwarzenegger nickname
47 Send to attack
48 Ideal places
50 Noodle variety
51 "Now you get to watch her leave out the window / Guess that's why they call it window ___" (Eminem lyric)
53 Entrepreneur's deg.
55 "IDGAF" singer Lipa

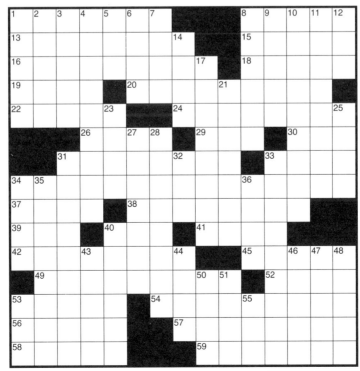

ANSWER, PAGE 92

ACROSS

1 Brand about which Dylan Mulvaney was speaking when she said that "to hire a trans person and then not publicly stand by them is worse, in my opinion, than not hiring a trans person at all"
9 Sister of Bella Hadid
13 Entice with
15 "What can I say?"
16 Canuck, e.g.
17 "Toy Story 3" bear
18 Not saying much
19 Footage taken from above, usually
21 Indian honorific
22 Prefix with "famous" or "matic"
23 Abbr. next to a number, maybe
24 "To this point ..."
27 Necessity for frying kleinur
30 "My Everything" artist Grande
34 Companion of the Tenth Doctor
35 Christmas(?) song with the lyric "Everyone hail to the pumpkin king"
39 Pound division

40 "What to choose, what to choose ..."
41 Many a family flick
43 Put out, as a statement
46 About to, briefly
47 Bakery fixtures
51 Toe beans' location
53 Renegade behaviour
55 Intrude, with "in"
57 Borders
58 Gossip spreader
60 "Be vewy vewy quiet" speaker
61 Made a value judgement about?
62 Long sandwiches with a name derived from a type of airship

63 Phenomenon that spawned competing hashtags: #whiteandgold, #blackandblue

DOWN

1 Taps gently, as a baseball
2 Brings (in)
3 Texas city whose name translates to "from the river"
4 Cats' resting places
5 Swallow Falls in "Cloudy with a Chance of Meatballs," e.g.
6 Handheld console of the '00s, briefly
7 Composer that sounds secretive?
8 Levels

9 Abandoned attractions
10 DJ Khaled hit in which Justin Bieber sings, "Yeah, you're sick of all those other imitators"
11 "Low on self-esteem, so you run on ___" (Halsey lyric)
12 Playing more for a win, briefly
14 Run like a deer
15 Flamenco shout
20 "I'll pass"
22 Fashion icon Apfel
25 Wows
26 Mermaid played by Halle Bailey
28 Febreze targets
29 Initials in old gamer "parties"
31 Tuna that's often seared

32 ___ June Paik, artist called "the father of video art"
33 "It's ___ Good!" (punny Spotify playlist name)
35 Leading
36 Like stuffed animals
37 Inelegant exposition delivery
38 Clark's love interest, in comics
42 ___ Eisley (setting for the "Star Wars" cantina scene)
44 Be part of a movement, say
45 Aerie residents
48 Fashion designer Wang
49 Laugh up a storm
50 Naiad in Greek mythology, e.g.
52 Puts two sheets together, maybe
53 Folk singer Joan whose name is worth 26 points in Scrabble (but it's not a legal word, so play ZABAJONE instead)
54 Member of a bygone "Union," for short
55 Nickname that omits "ley" or "ford"
56 Jake and ___ (comedy duo)
59 Speckled gray blocks, in Minecraft

ANSWER, PAGE 92

57

ACROSS

1 Bubble machine?
11 Train for the ring
15 Exclusive, in a way
16 Dance accompanying mele
17 "Major kudos"
18 ___ mess (fruity dessert originating from an English college)
19 Die down
21 Not a party person?: Abbr.
22 Nowhere to be found
24 Chickpea, by another name
26 Makes a smooth pass
29 Organic food label
30 They're all charged up
31 Pinky swear, e.g.
33 New start?
34 Piece in a solitaire game
35 Barhop, maybe
37 Browser division
40 "Kill Bill" singer
42 Coming-out phrase
43 Leave at the altar
44 Rolling requirements
47 Team involved in Deflategate
49 Early release of a video game

51 "What? How could you get that wrong?"
52 Comfy shoe, casually
53 Write for a living, in slang
56 Elegant bend
58 Protector of YouTube commentary videos
62 "Ageless" skin care brand
63 Pick-me-up request
64 Sauce on some enchiladas
65 Path of least resistance?

DOWN

1 Character with a crystal above its head
2 With 3-Down, burned, say
3 See 2-Down
4 Devices designed to be sweat-resistant
5 Surname in a best-selling 2011 erotic romance novel
6 Word in the name of an experimental file
7 Dog toy material
8 Their CEOs are in power
9 Foil company
10 "I'll go now"
11 Dodie song with the lyric "Am I allowed to look at her like that?"
12 Start
13 Comedian Bodden
14 Unknown people, slangily

20 Troy: "How did you know my nickname was ___?" Jeff: "Because you're a football player and your name begins with 'T'": "Community"
22 "Need some ___ for that burn?"
23 Sports bar selling point, maybe
25 Tinder bio info
26 Taste tester's amount
27 Hotel amenity that's a great way to ... wait, it costs HOW much just to have someone put hot stones on my back?
28 Saxophone variety, briefly

32 Instrument similar to a euphonium
35 Pasta, bread, etc.
36 Employ a giant beanbag, say
38 Saxophone variety
39 ___ Meal (onetime stan-oriented McDonald's offering)
41 Calm
43 Simple Minds' lead vocalist
44 Tail on a craft Easter Bunny, maybe
45 Last word in the title of many concert albums recorded in Harlem
46 Post with a "might delete later" caption, sometimes
48 Charges
50 Disney role for Anika Noni Rose
54 Surname in a best-selling 2011 erotic romance novel
55 Some contraceptives
57 Look at
59 It's embarrassing to be caught in one
60 Nickname that omits "laide"
61 ___-Nap

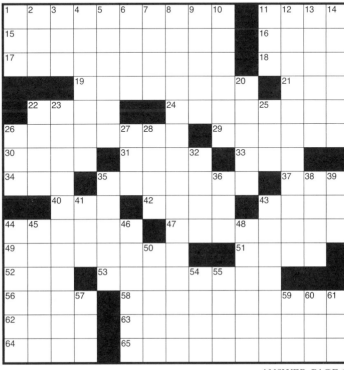

ANSWER, PAGE 93

58

ACROSS

1 Touch grass, so to speak
7 "Live ___" (Taco Bell slogan)
10 Responsible partiers, briefly
13 Tehran-based carrier
15 Avatar on Apple devices
17 Implore
18 DC supervillain (a.k.a. Charles Brown) who travels by gliding and, yes, is named after the "Peanuts" character
19 Dotted lines?
20 Filling with joy
21 Course figures
23 Logic Pro plug-in, e.g.
25 Triple threat's quality
26 Forwarded, e.g.
27 Make an oopsie
29 Lacking
30 "STOP with this DISRESPECT"
35 Where many bend over backwards to participate?
37 Nonexistent neighborhood in "Don't Stop Believin'"
40 Part of a Batman outfit
43 Family guy?
44 "Hedwig and the Angry ___"
45 Dissolving liquids
47 Like, fancily
49 Jam band Umphrey's ___
50 Not a coincidence
52 Cut off
54 "Children of Blood and Bone" author Tomi
55 Some Broadway tributes
58 Spanish "My God!"
59 Train component
60 Train stop: Abbr.
61 Missouri-based hub, briefly
62 Feature of a luxurious resort

DOWN

1 Women's ___
2 Aluminum container?
3 What carpoolers chip in for
4 Time when everything seems to go wrong
5 Nonbinary possessive
6 Fan-written works, for short
7 Fill with joy
8 Kapoor of "Slumdog Millionaire"
9 Its name comes from the Persian for "three strings" (though it has more now)
10 Name for a black-and-white cat
11 "Unchained" character in a 2012 film
12 FKA Twigs, e.g.
14 Large flightless bird
16 "Oh, when you said your Aunt Flo was visiting, I assumed you were speaking ___. Nice to meet you, Flo"
21 Trident-shaped letter
22 Power (up)
24 E-cig accessory
28 Unlikely to make a good first impression
31 In the past
32 Smear
33 Medication nicknamed "Fem & M's"
34 "Scram!"
36 Numbers that might be given to a crush, maybe?
38 See 39-Down
39 With 38-Down, something broken at parties
40 Beetle spots, e.g.
41 Passed the test with flying colors
42 Join in the criticism
46 Originates (from)
48 Whispering letters?
49 Word before "blitz" or "circus"
51 Put out
53 Leave, with "out"
56 Pay up?
57 Spanish "madam": Abbr.

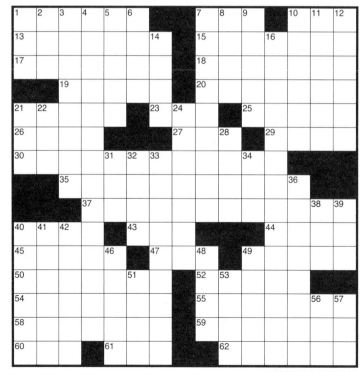

ANSWER, PAGE 93

59

ACROSS

1 Attacked
7 "Can you believe that cameo!?!?"
15 Greek muse of astronomy
16 "It's got a kick to it!"
17 Coke Zero competitor
18 Failed attempt at virality
19 Humble response to "They're gonna love it"
21 Move, briefly
22 Business ___ (entrepreneur's quality)
23 Essay premise
25 Possible response to "Any restrictions?"
27 Billboard award whose winners include Prince, Cher, Pink, and many artists with last names as well
28 Fifth month, in 11-Down
29 Sped-up music genre
34 Part of UAE
36 "The Metamorphosis" protagonist
37 The Balloon Boy incident, e.g.
38 "Please stop"
40 Its famous "Tour" is a different org. altogether
41 Obligation
42 Crash or Eddie, e.g., in "Ice Age"
46 Like "Elden Ring" or "Grand Theft Auto V"
49 From an elite school
50 Retailer whose name rhymes with "satay sauce"
51 After the next revolution
53 Made like Bolt and bolted
55 Wiggle
59 Family member who's prone to snap?
60 Schafer of "Euphoria"
61 Act start
62 "Gadzooks!"

DOWN

1 Chew on this!
2 Journalist Drennen
3 Jemison on the Space Shuttle Endeavor
4 Lure
5 Distant "embrace"
6 Washington city
7 "___ Talking" (2022 film)
8 Gardening tools
9 "Mmm, that makes sense"
10 Airport org.
11 Class where "tout le monde" may be greeted
12 Last name of rapper Cam'ron
13 Cause for recalls
14 Too and to, for two?
20 Flag shop purchase
22 Birdy?
24 See 57-Down
25 Computer that was a part of the "clear craze"
26 Rooney of "The Girl With the Dragon Tattoo"
27 Place for Boomerangs, briefly
30 "Personally," in texts
31 "___-daisy!"
32 Meat sauce
33 Crammer's concern
35 Intentionally
36 Enter, as an art contest
39 Its 2023 additions include "frontstabbing," "flirtationship," and "final frontier": Abbr.
43 Preferring single-person bathrooms, likely
44 Not transparent
45 Originated
46 Harsh voice qualities
47 Umbrella term that includes demi and graysexual orientations, for short
48 Patisserie offering
49 One called "jefe," maybe
52 Light gas
54 Scots denial
56 "How was ___ know that?"
57 With 24-Down, difficult to touch?
58 "___ Kormel is Not Normal!" ("My Weird School" book)

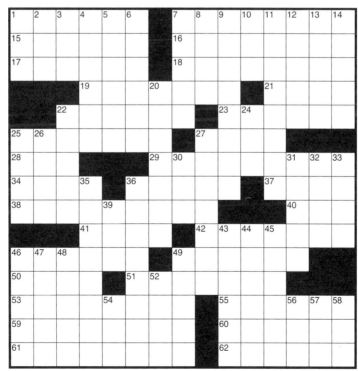

ANSWER, PAGE 93

65

60

ACROSS

1 Texting tech, for short
4 Certain postgrad degree
7 "Got any ___ 4 where 2 eat when I'm in NYC?"
11 Jazz base
12 "___, and" (improv tenet)
13 Dad's follow-up to his kids' "iPod" and "iPad," in an old viral image
15 Corny headwear?
17 British series set on its titular "Street," to fans
19 Eugene's state: Abbr.
20 Nonhuman identities
22 "The ___ is not your friend": Stephen King in "On Writing"
24 They're really deep
25 Website that collects histories of Internet jokes
27 Remove soap from
28 High-speed ___
29 Zach or Cody, e.g., in "The Suite Life of Zach and Cody"
33 "___ have said before ..."
34 Quick back-and-forths?
37 Having 4 sharps, say
38 Tired
40 Call up
41 Smartphone precursor
43 "This place isn't like it used to be"
46 Addressed
49 Harbinger
50 Output of many a YouTuber
52 Descriptor for some hair
54 Marriages, e.g.
55 Shallow marine habitat
57 Lean on the pedal
58 Now, in Italian
59 ___ as shootin'
60 Prozac and Estradiol, e.g., for short
61 Prefix for "duck," in "Pokémon"
62 Was an avid consumer, perhaps?

DOWN

1 Pho ingredient
2 North ___ (Balkan country)
3 "They can't know we're here"
4 "Thanks for saving me!"
5 Wraps rich in protein
6 Regarding
7 Southern region of the United States
8 Namesake
9 Tarot deck, e.g.
10 Paddock pops
11 Card game with "Flip!," "Flex!," and "All Wild!" variants
14 Extremely serious
16 Some daisies
18 One of three in Sussex?
21 Parts of Twitch stream setups, often
23 Golfs with drivers?
25 Krusty ___ ("SpongeBob" restaurant)
26 Pours out?
30 Manage to leave a tight space
31 "This isn't enough"
32 Weird Al character in a "Ridin'" parody
35 What morps (a.k.a anti-proms) may be held as
36 Few and far between
39 "Help yourself"
42 Suffix for "Disney"
44 Soviet leader Brezhnev
45 Highest point
46 "Law and Order: ___"
47 Send a notification to
48 Unwavering hatred
51 "I have had enough!"
53 Shout that might punctuate a flamenco
56 Letters in an educational tweet, perhaps

ANSWER, PAGE 93

61

ACROSS

1 "We'll figure this out," more concisely
4 See as more than a friend?
8 Ink pouch
11 Haul ass
12 Word before "horizon" or "space"
14 "Just jokin' around"
15 "... among others": Abbr.
16 People whose lifestyles allow for great mobility
19 Sitting on, say
21 Prozac's company
22 "502 Bad Gateway," e.g.
25 Like the least believable Bigfoot photos
26 Group that sounds like a part of paparazzi?
28 The members of Citi Zēni (who finished 14th out of 17 at Eurovision 2022 with "Eat Your Salad," and they were ROBBED), e.g.
29 Made aware
31 ___Express (China-based retail service)
32 Minecraft item made with gunpowder and sand
33 It dropped its optional essay section in 2021
36 Prefix with "pronoun"
37 ___ McCallion, Ada Rook's partner in the band Black Dresses
39 Not standard
41 Religious offshoot
43 First to join an arcade game
44 Mobile game where movements of shapes are synced with music
46 Technicians on a tour
47 Musical hit
49 Horror with no grounds in reality?
52 Game that cannot tell you to use the +4 card differently than you've been using it all this time (it can't)
53 Word in many Shrek puns
54 "___ what I was thinking ..."
55 House in "House," and others: Abbr.
56 The Plufl is a human-sized one based on a common purchase for dogs
57 Nintendo ___ (handheld consoles)
58 Key out?

DOWN

1 ___ Queen (Speedy's alter ego on "Arrow")
2 Amber drinks
3 "It's ___ Season, Motherf***ers" (online essay with the line "Guess what season it is— f***ing fall")
4 Game programmer, briefly
5 "Colin in Black & White" co-creator DuVernay
6 Urban housing
7 Happening all the time
8 Phoebe Bridgers outfit
9 Cake texture descriptor
10 Music collectibles, for short
13 Loosen, maybe
14 Achieved through vile means
17 Pro golfer Ernie
18 Knave, in logic puzzles
20 IRL-friends-only account, say
23 "I got that covered"
24 "Glass Onion" director Johnson
25 "I'm so ___!"
27 Necessity for kitchen work
30 Serve, with "out"
33 All of the films in its main saga were nominated for Academy Awards
34 "Niiiice"
35 Covered in streaks of white, say
38 Climbing tool
39 Changed slightly
40 Nest eggs for many
42 Checklist header
43 Western Australian capital
45 Stark franchise, for short
46 ___ Against the Machine
48 D'Anjou alternative
49 ___ watch
50 "Why golly!"
51 5 on a calculator, maybe

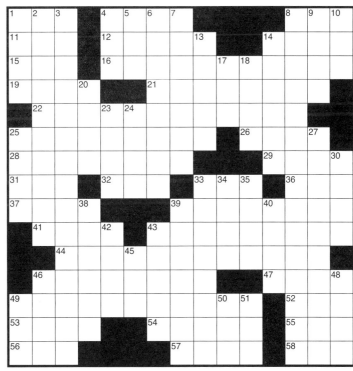

ANSWER, PAGE 94

62

ACROSS

1 Double Big ___ (Canadian sandwiches)
5 Movie ranking org.
8 Tries to find, with "for"
13 Something caught after a controversial statement
14 Mitochondria, for the cell
17 Encyclopedia SpongeBobia, e.g.
18 Clif product
19 "Breaking Bad" stuff
21 Trumpet accessories
22 Letters on block packaging
23 Disappear
25 Quiet part of a conversation
26 Org. whose deadline may make you feel like you can't wait five days to get to 4/20
27 Clichéd movie trailer phrase
29 Shine like a certain surgical instrument
31 OB-___
32 Not being serious
35 Online literacy promoter?
36 Spine components
37 Biter in "Cleopatra"
40 "My bread went bad, but it's ___-refundable" (pun)
41 2010s YouTube scandal named after a "Frozen" character
43 Looking pale
44 Sit next to
47 F equivalent
48 Had
49 Real large estate
51 Talking bear of a 2010 film
52 Tap
55 Click the floppy disk icon
57 Approaching a deadline fast
58 Workers whose first letter stands for "Treasury"
59 Make law
60 Talking bear of a 2012 film
61 Press enter on

DOWN

1 Abbr. accompanying a reaction image
2 Separation cost
3 Where the batter gets baked
4 Method some choose for getting dragged in the winter
5 Java product
6 Intake sheet, e.g.
7 "Those are long odds"
8 "Don't worry, it isn't hard"
9 Period lasting forever, seemingly
10 Eat exclusively, with "on"
11 "Skip the line" option at airports, familiarly
12 Feudal laborers
15 "I expected this from them ... but YOU?"
16 Instagram's equivalent to a TikTok
20 It'll stick out on a fancy car
23 Show for a comic, e.g.
24 ___ Loops
28 When repeated, crush on
30 iPad model
33 Any of Gru's daughters, as he would say it
34 Degrade
35 Arthur of "The Golden Girls"
36 Zac's co-star in "High School Musical"
37 Big-budget FPS, e.g., in industry slang
38 Endeavored (to)
39 Focus of some rallies
40 Source of pride, maybe
42 Blinky, Pinky, Inky, and Clyde, e.g.
43 Pixar character whose name is an acronym
45 When repeated, a Jessie J hit
46 Meter or inch, e.g.
50 Italian capital
53 Speech habit
54 ___ Flanders, inspiration for the heavy metal band Okilly Dokilly
56 Anagram of 54-Down

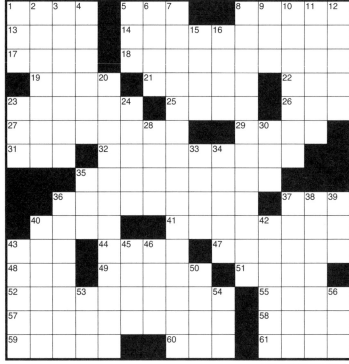

ANSWER, PAGE 94

63

ACROSS

1 Put in the work (for)
7 A Dorian equivalent
13 "Christmas With the Kranks" extra
14 Show more skin, maybe?
15 Aware of
16 Hosted a conference, maybe
17 Moved furtively, as a cat
18 In short ___ (how work may be accomplished)
19 Reluctantly handed (over)
20 Equine Pokémon that evolves into Rapidash
21 More mocking, as humor
22 "I need a hug right now"
23 Deal
24 Cry about wealth inequality?
28 ___ B. Wells (2020 Pulitzer Prize citation recipient, posthumously)
29 Singer with the 2019 hit "Prom Dress"
30 "All-American Girl" comedian Margaret
31 Closing, as a drop-down menu
33 ___ jacket
34 Subscription perks, on Twitch
35 Instrument not generally played in marching bands for obvious reasons
36 Comes to an end
37 Nonsense
38 Subject of Wikipedia's "Association football" entry
39 Back
40 His in Hawaii?
41 Revealed
42 Suffering the most from Zumba, maybe
43 Every now and then
44 Not as much
45 Put on a ___ (dunk on, in slang)

DOWN

1 Onion-y?
2 Tchotchke
3 Chair that encourages leaning
4 "Psych!"
5 Respond to orders, in a way?
6 Unit from the Greek for "work"
7 Animal also called a whistle-pig
8 Robin Hood group
9 "Repertoire" comedian James
10 Volkswagen compact car
11 Pindaric ___ (historical celebration pieces)
12 Color of the crewmate who, stereotypically, is always accused of being the impostor in Among Us
13 "Good Luck Charlie" setting
15 OnlyFans offering
18 "Michael ___ Big, Sexy Valentine's Day Special" (2017 Netflix variety show)
20 Subjects of some books for toddlers
22 Animal that a ZhuZhu Pet is modeled after
24 Shows, as something new
25 Any member of Eurovision's Daði og Gagnamagnið, e.g.
26 Cups in optical illusions
27 Feeling the love, say
29 Singer of 1969's "It's Getting Better"
32 Moochers, dramatically
33 Seine-timental way to say "I love you"?
35 Slow-cooked meal
36 Beer brand based in 13-Down
37 "Any ___?" ("Throw me a bone here, I'm completely stuck")
38 Ingredient in a Slow Negroni
39 Pic of Pamplona
40 System in which pretending to cradle a baby means "baby": Abbr.
41 Top that's always getting twisted around

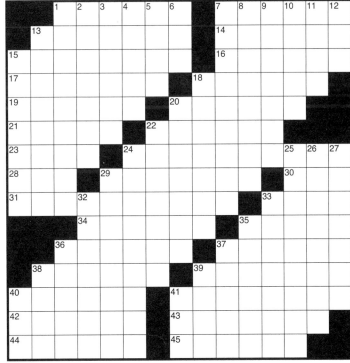

ANSWER, PAGE 94

64

ACROSS

1 Ten-dollar bills, in old slang
9 Big name in banks or bikes
13 "It's 1 A.M., why is this person texting me?"
15 Oodles
16 Song set to kinetic typography
17 French military cap
18 Landed
19 They often seem too good to be true
20 "Good Girls Revolt" actress Darke
21 Huge expanse
22 "No no no, you're completely right"
24 "I laugh in your face at such a suggestion!"
25 "No ice"... or "Noice!"
26 Equipment aimed at reporters, often
32 Rank below S, on Internet lists
35 Many look to confirm it
36 Word after "close-up" or "movie"
38 Reusable bag
39 Sheet material
41 They hire people to find work
43 Puts on years
45 Chilly remark
46 "Sorry, what? Our connection is bad"
51 Sus alternative, in chords
54 Fashion house name
55 "One L" author Scott
56 Treated spots
57 Playwright whose name can be found in "writing exercise"
58 Like, fine, I guess
60 It may be subjective or objective
61 Successful children of successful people, slangily
62 "Diary of a Wimpy Kid" protagonist
63 Barren

DOWN

1 Put up, as locks?
2 Rooms where the sun beams in
3 Not one ___
4 ___ for Her (bygone pen brand)
5 Conflict where we're the good guys, obviously
6 Girl, in Spanish
7 Polaroid alternative
8 "My bad, don't care"
9 Sprinkles might be added directly into it
10 New software version
11 Trending thing
12 Penned
13 "But ___ ..." ("However ...")
14 Violin bow application
22 Jokey response to "Nobody's perfect"
23 Chatime product
24 Indonesian fried rice dish
26 "American Dad!" channel
27 By way of
28 Listing of BBC programmes, e.g.
29 Gandhi protested it
30 Gone by
31 Fam member
33 Abbr. for the unlisted?
34 Daisy Ridley's "Star Wars" role
37 Rhyming tequila brand
40 "We're like your ___ game, 'cause we can't be beat!" ("Artists vs. TMNT" rap battle lyric)
42 The "Me" in "Despicable Me"
44 Occupy, as a beanbag chair
46 Checking to see if someone's a 47-Down
47 One barred from a bar
48 Put in the microwave
49 Crush flavor
50 Toys dating back to the 5th century BCE
51 Crush the exam
52 "I wish I could ___ that"
53 Opens on Hanukkah, say
56 "Waterloo" band
59 "She's So High" singer Bachman

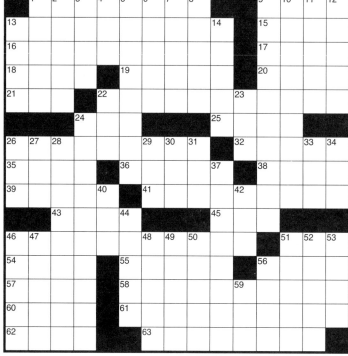

ANSWER, PAGE 94

65

ACROSS

1 Bisected
6 Last word of some silent films
9 Droop
12 Polynesian sarong
13 Letterless number, on keypads
14 "This doesn't ___ to me"
16 Google Drive file, perhaps
17 Hitting hard
18 More likely to bet on it
19 The cool kids might have their own spot on it
20 Lil Nas X game where you are encouraged to shake to "Montero" songs
22 Mars of Silk Sonic

24 Where "you are," on maps
25 "Sounds fun!"
26 Body of eau
27 Oman neighbor: Abbr.
29 D.C. agency whose seal includes a windmill and lightning bolt
31 Time to expose one's arms?
36 Elvis's Scatter, e.g.
38 "Yadda yadda yadda"
40 Legal suffix
41 ___ feed
42 Unsatisfying ending
43 "I relate to this so much"
46 Part of STEAM, for short
49 Looking to buy, say

51 Tired (of)
53 Optimist's word
54 Blender setting
55 "Unholy" singer Smith
56 "That's unpleasant"
59 Components of some breakdowns?
60 Children might wait for one
61 Possible follow-up to "Any takers?"
62 As of now
63 Guitarist Paul
64 "Commit tax fraud" and others

DOWN

1 Some online "addresses"
2 "Eh, I don't feel like it"

3 Font "launched" by Microsoft in 1996
4 Li'l bairn
5 Sends elsewhere, as jobs
6 How Mario Party 8 and 9 were exclusively released
7 Astounded
8 Shinier, so to speak
9 Binge
10 Having drunk lots of coffee, say
11 Greek street food
14 Request
15 "Pssssh"
21 Sale sights, sometimes
22 Sandwich with guac, in some queer cafes
23 Grating noise
28 Runner, e.g.

30 Jokey term for the instant between making a huge mistake and realizing it
32 Binding words?
33 E-commerce center?
34 "Spa" and "ahhh," e.g., per this book
35 Up against
37 "Artemis Fowl" author Colfer
39 "You're prettier than usual," e.g.
43 ___ atinlay
44 It'll stop a fight
45 Deserve
47 Stand up for arts education?
48 Want
50 Website with a yodeled jingle
52 "Asteroid City" director Anderson
57 Guelph's province: Abbr.
58 Nickname that omits "mond"

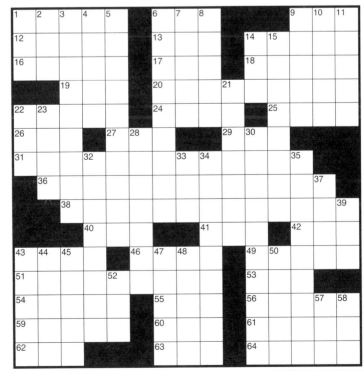

ANSWER, PAGE 95

71

66

ACROSS

1 Domino's Tracker page feature
4 Shows affection toward, say
8 "Sounds fun!"
12 Jughead's orientation in the comics, for short
13 Go up against
14 O'Brien who "Needs a Friend," per his podcast
16 How ramblers don't talk
18 "Hey, dude!"
19 Colgate competitor
20 Two in a Crayola 24-count box
22 "From our perspective ..."
23 Jones or Davidson, e.g.
25 Getting word?
27 Euphoric-sounding rock band
28 2008 memoir that's all "Mee, Mee, Mee"?
31 Personal polygraphs?
34 Timmy Turner, to Vicky on "The Fairly OddParents"
35 Felt remorse about
36 Advertiser's concern
39 "You make a good point"
40 "This is icon behavior"
42 Guelph ___ (mythologically named Ontario athletes)
44 "You're catching my drift"
47 Up to
48 Stein filler
49 Hamiltons
53 Willing and ___
55 Something taken with caution?
57 Nintendo song that introduces, among others, Diddy and Chunky
58 "That's sick!"
60 Upgrade in a fast-food combo
62 The most expensive item ever sold on eBay (for $168 million!)
63 Didn't rule out
64 Busy beaver's project
65 Pueblo people
66 Summer quality
67 Hosp. areas

DOWN

1 It runs Pro applications
2 Scrat's pursuit
3 ___ code
4 They take tips: Abbr.
5 Sister album to "Folklore," in Taylor Swift's discography
6 Tall ___
7 Cunning sort
8 Unfit for skateboarding, e.g.
9 Debatable
10 State of having no unreads
11 Anime-inspired sprint that's, ironically, slower than regular sprinting
13 Small cut of meat
15 Snipes without a guide, in a video game
17 Attacked with catlike reflexes?
21 "Don't tell them our secrets!"
24 Prefix like super-
26 Mel of baseball
29 Dictionaries weigh in on it
30 "Gee, that's so sweet"
31 Murphy of "Clueless"
32 Vessel for nigiri and sashimi
33 "Master of Puppets" band
37 Rubric contents
38 Jekyll counterpart
41 Intelligence org.
43 Remained unresolved, as a patent application
45 They don't want no scrubs
46 Hearts may represent it
50 Break down
51 Release ___ (Spotify feature)
52 DDOSes, e.g.
54 Publicly share, as sentiments
56 Like valuable Pokémon cards
59 Aliens, for short
61 Part of WYSIWYG

ANSWER, PAGE 95

67

ACROSS

1 Part of a pronoun duo
4 "That'd be nice"
9 Marvel actor's crowd, often
14 "___ is me!"
15 Kids' plea to parents
16 A ticket for it likely won't get you anywhere
17 UFO crew
18 Remove from the top of one's profile
19 Gets pwned, say
20 "___ Bird Now" (Anohni and the Johnsons album)
22 Bit of weed (or breaded chicken), casually
23 They're checked at checkups
24 Reaches for
26 Sloth, e.g.
27 "Rio" bird
28 Big cheese
29 Binary address
30 Electronic drum kit sound
31 Time of little hope
34 Not fitting in a binary
35 Source of animated reactions
36 ___ dog (vegan entrée)
37 Dorm area, casually
38 Hawaiian celebration on May 1st
42 Become inedible
43 That guy's
44 "No more stalling"
45 Annie's last name on "Community"
47 Match ender, briefly
48 Pivot on an axis
49 Runway sight
50 Not including
52 ___ text (accessibility feature)
53 Without breaks
54 Cute laugh feature
55 Item often printed on demand
56 First impressions, e.g.
57 Up on the latest stories
58 Ticket info, briefly

DOWN

1 "Anchors ___!"
2 Comedian Tig
3 Unwavering supporter
4 Critical care dept.
5 "I'm craving takeout. You?"
6 HDMI cable for a monitor, e.g.
7 Quick drink
8 Lady Kluck in Disney's "Robin Hood," e.g.
9 Risky way to go
10 Contents of an online gambler's "crate"
11 "I remember nothing, really"
12 Incredible
13 "Wheel of Fortune" segment
21 Gayle hit that incorporates the alphabet
23 Realty website offerings
25 Cut of beef
26 Artist whose "Thong Song" was covered in a baffling "Glee" sequence
29 Belgradians, e.g.
30 Collabs on a Google Doc together, say
32 "Flowers for Algernon" author
33 "___ my plan ..."
34 Listing on many a Christmastime Buzzfeed article
35 "Funny!"
36 Quake
39 Grow, as pupils
40 Charm
41 Threw, as an empty water bottle
43 Doesn't leak
44 "You've told me this before"
46 Relay, as a meme
47 Sharp point
50 Portal with a butterfly logo
51 Piggy's spot

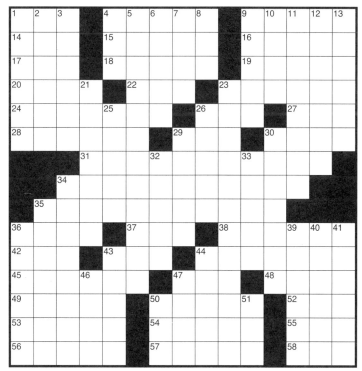

ANSWER, PAGE 95

73

68

ACROSS

1 Dressing areas?
10 Maple products
14 2007 flop with the tagline "We Know It's Big. We Measured."
15 Oolong onomatopoeia
16 Craves affection, like a kitty
17 Delta, e.g.
18 Doc ___ (Spider-Man foe, informally)
19 Products in overly specific Facebook ads, often
20 Turn into wallets, as empty Kool-Aid Jammer pouches, say
21 "Mouth Dreams" artist Cicierega
23 Like some work training
25 Letters before BC?
26 "Ain't that something!"
28 Symbol of strength
29 Common guy-to-guy greeting
30 "keeping it 100 ..."
31 Transcendent state
33 "My Favourite Faded Fantasy" artist Rice
36 "Microcosmos" love scene pair
37 It'll help bring some color to the face
38 They might smooth things unnecessarily
39 Delta Air Lines hub, briefly
40 Soak (up)
41 "Gimme the ___"
43 Desire, like money?
44 Stood with arms outstretched
46 Goals
49 Pizza portion
51 Feature of a Sphynx or lynx, but not a Manx
52 "Don't Start Now" artist Lipa
53 "El ___: The Adventures of Manny Rivera" (Nickelodeon show)
54 [buzzer sound]
57 Hardly zeitgeisty
58 "Neon Future" DJ
59 They're off when things get unpredictable
60 Tracked

DOWN

1 Install, as a button?
2 Swiftly
3 ___ Park ("Numb" guys)
4 Overcome procrastination
5 Slide into someone's ___
6 "High School Musical" song whose title precedes "Slip and slide and ride that rhythm"
7 Eczema Therapy brand
8 Brises and others
9 Jams, e.g.
10 Blueberry lookalike
11 Like crisp leaves in warm colors
12 Some false nails
13 Packetful in a breakfast diner
15 Surprisingly popular ogre-themed party event
22 "Don't you worry about it"
24 Soft Cell hit with the lyric "I've got to get away"
27 Hard to justify, pricing-wise
32 XP successor
33 It often provides the where and when, in news articles
34 Until the morning
35 "You gotta hand it to the kids" mentality?
37 Proof of work, often
41 Covered in salt, say
42 Like profile photos?
45 Mass delusion that the media DOESN'T want to talk about
47 Faffs (about)
48 Composer Erik ___ (born Eric ___)
50 Sports broadcaster Collinsworth
55 Thing in a courtroom?
56 ___ Dunn (often-imitated pottery brand)

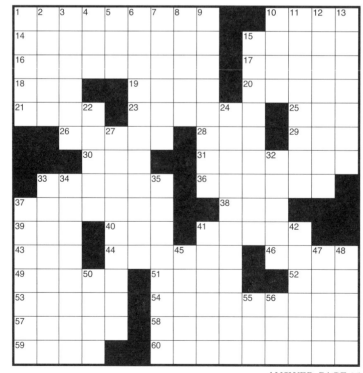

ANSWER, PAGE 95

69

ACROSS

1 Shaming syllable
4 Neck accessory
8 App with Reels, casually
13 Fish that sounds like a Greek shout
15 Kingly Norwegian name
16 Come together to make
17 Common chess puzzle
19 Naomi of the Women's Tennis Association
20 2022 Record of the Year winners
22 Only visible features of a cartoon character in the dark, often
23 "Smart" guy
24 Dribs and ___
26 Uncomfortable bed material
29 You guys'
31 Stereotypical clown name
34 Land of ___ ("Adventure Time" setting)
35 Converses, e.g.
37 "Had to be there, really"
40 Joins, as a tournament
41 Comedian Amuquandoh of "This Hour Has 22 Minutes"
42 Opposite of "admit"
43 Fighting
44 Boxing Day events
46 Man in Nintendo Land?
48 Work before a restaurant's opening, briefly
50 Below-knee?
52 Designs meant to be hung up
56 Highly reluctant
58 Twice-worshipping group, perhaps?
60 Volunteer's offer
61 Some contraceptives
62 Cool off on a summer's day, maybe
63 Some of their products suck but they have lots of fans
64 Words famously belted by Whitney Houston
65 "I'm good, dude"

DOWN

1 Part of a drum kit
2 Centers focused on Ayurveda, maybe
3 Winter of "Sleepy Hollow"
4 Hip-hop offshoot focused on educating and uplifting
5 Sax type
6 Piece in a Sicilian Defense opening
7 Eggy?
8 "Sweet dreams are made of cheese / Who am ___ diss a Brie?"
9 They're pretty high (though rarely in price)
10 Works overtime, perhaps
11 Yoink, say
12 "Unfortunately"
14 Protest chant
18 Blåhaj seller
21 Drink marketed with the slogan "You've never seen a taste like this"
25 Character with an arrowhead?
27 ___ Surprise! (big-eyed doll brand)
28 Combo drinks, often
30 Potato part used in appetizers
31 "Peace!"
32 Chaplin of the upcoming third "Avatar" film
33 Calls from your seat?
36 Room that's hardly kempt
38 Spoken
39 Sports org. whose players are featured in the Wordle-inspired game Poeltl
45 Goofs up
47 Finnish cellphone maker
49 Seafood serving
50 Caught some ice
51 Word before "cannoli" or "cow"
53 Partook in web development?
54 "Sweeney ___"
55 Miller of "The Haunting of Bly Manor"
57 Sweetie
59 "For shame," in texts

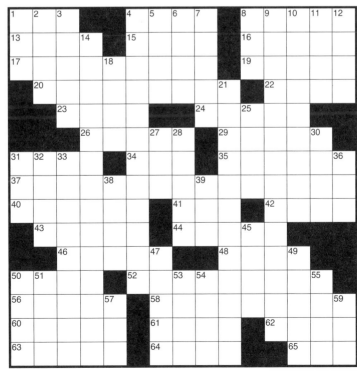

ANSWER, PAGE 96

75

ACROSS

1 Not available worldwide

11 Fanfic trope set in a different reality in which, say, Spock might be a barista and Kirk might be his customer

13 E-tail offerings (and where "ETAIL" can be found backwards)

15 Gosling/Stone film of 2016

16 Harder to watch around family members, likely

17 Drawer collection

18 Model Holliday

19 Big name in champagne

20 Adoption process?

26 Got ___ (scored highly)

27 Like some knowledge

28 2010s-era meme videos with airhorns, no-scopes, and techno music

33 "This is so FRUSTRAT-ING"

34 Administrator of fueleconomy.gov, briefly

37 Seeks help from, as a star

39 Common pie filling

40 Asked for a card from, say

42 "We Are One (___)" (2014 FIFA World Cup anthem by Pitbull)

44 Not giving the truth?

47 Taken

49 "Singles only"

51 One responding well to a callback, maybe

52 Wading through

DOWN

1 Zoom

2 Fill in online forms

3 From not too long ago

4 "Just because you're a lesbian, it doesn't make you less of a ___'" (words of support from Marge Simpson, queer ally)

5 Open (with)

6 Abbr. on albums with track titles like "Closing Credits"

7 Chaz's mother

8 Nut whose extract is no longer used in its most popular namesake drink

9 Total legend, say?

10 He was "back at it again with the white Vans," in a meme

11 Toronto Argonauts, e.g.

12 Instruments made by Kamaka or Lanikai, informally

13 "Molly's Game" director Sorkin

14 "r u being ___??"

15 Buddhist monk

21 "What a steal!"

22 Hangry feelings

23 Prefix meaning "straight"

24 ___ de las chichas (yo, por ejemplo)

25 Person born around early winter, casually

29 Didn't hold back

30 Amenity at a rest stop (and 25-Down backwards)

31 ___-jongg

32 What you can't do to the person standing in front of you at a concert, often

35 Having left the house less often, say

36 Just ___ (not too much)

37 Comment after a fall, maybe

38 Airplane wing label (good to know)

39 The Icelandic folklore creatures "marbendlar," e.g.

40 "That applies to me"

41 "Bummer"

43 McCord portrayer in "Madam Secretary"

45 Junction

46 Force outside?

47 It's not straight

48 Haim on the bass

50 El ___ (Castilian knight)

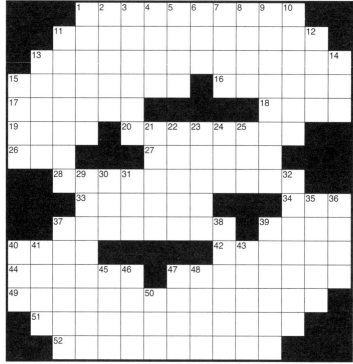

ANSWER, PAGE 96

71

ACROSS

1 "That went way over my head"
14 "What's the harm in 30 extra minutes?"
15 Ben & Jerry's flavor with Jimmy Fallon on the packaging
16 Spacetime disturbances
17 Comedian Drew
18 ___ Speedwagon
19 Delfino of "Super Mario Sunshine," e.g.
20 T-shaped contraceptive
21 Prepare some Kool-Aid, say
22 Help get to the bottom of things?
26 Canadian pianist Gould
27 Permit
28 Tray contents
30 ___ al-Fitr
31 Exam that some people always get an A on?
33 Stan or Spike of movies
34 "You wanna know how I got these ___?"
35 TV Guide abbr.
38 Metallic impact sound
40 Slim cookie
42 Work on, as a talent
43 Take off the table
45 "Pardon?," humorously
46 See 44-Down
47 Father John ___
49 Papers for a pad?
50 Shows after a long break
53 Auto shop purchases
54 Birthday centers?

DOWN

1 Like Elton John's "Your Song," keywise
2 Made, after expenses
3 Semordnilap of some word in this clue
4 Jorgen ___ Strangle of "The Fairly OddParents"
5 Accompanier of Tim bits?
6 Came back into power
7 Jacket type for Dr. Evil
8 Had 38-Down, with "for"
9 All in order
10 "Looking for," on dating apps
11 Sent flowers, say
12 Arrive surreptitiously
13 Render (less) harmless, as a bull
14 "That tracks"
15 Warble
21 Something made for a quick dinner?
23 "Doctor Who" enemy
24 When repeated, rock band whose name … bears repeating?
25 "___ the lucky girl?"
26 Painter's base
29 Hollywood sidewalk sight
31 Well, in Rome
32 ___ Perez, makeup brand whose second name contains its first
33 A whiiiiile back
35 Stymies, as a scheme
36 Info on a famous media chart
37 Ponies (up)
38 See 8-Down
39 "Hustlers" director Scafaria
41 Fin
43 Psychologist Alfred
44 46-Across with famous Sarah McLachlan commercials
47 First word of the title by which "La Gioconda" is better known
48 "My fingies!"
49 Dramatic yell in a courtroom
51 Part of SOHCAHTOA: Abbr.
52 Format for many English essays: Abbr.

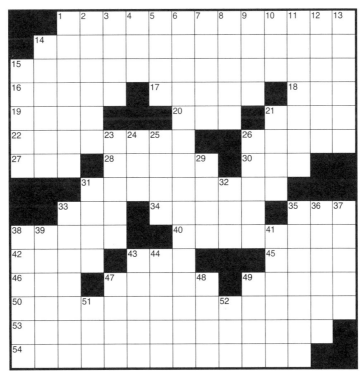

ANSWER, PAGE 96

72

ACROSS

1 Cause trouble
10 Something "broken" in the morning
14 Ice bath activity
15 E, in the NATO alphabet
16 Form of cute vandalism involving googly craft supplies
17 [Raises hand]
18 Like the tree branch Thorin used as a shield, in Tolkien lore
19 Guy friends, in French
20 Periodontist's concern
21 Enjoys the snowy weather, say
22 ___ positive
23 Concering, briefly
24 Merchandise
26 "You can click the link, Dad"
29 Adjective with a silent letter
30 Gets one's hair styled, maybe
31 38-Down, e.g.
34 Some origami creations
36 Starts making sense
37 Glacier relatives
39 It has the face of a baby in "Teletubbies"
41 Excessively
42 Common mystery movie setting
44 Robert De ___ of "The Irishman"
45 Old Nintendo handheld, briefly
47 Crows
50 ___ above
51 Look all over the playground, say
52 Ali in the ring
53 Hang ___
54 Start of a childish taunt
56 It might start with a germ
57 Common airport amenity
58 Many a comedy event, for short
59 "Who wants to do it?"

DOWN

1 Descriptor for the Game of Ur, one of the world's oldest board games
2 Beer barrel
3 "Sounds fun!"
4 Many YouTube videos have one
5 Furniture wood
6 Havana residents
7 Genre for "My Hero Academia" or ... (checks Google) "Ben 10"
8 Risky place to leave your car keys unattended
9 Darkroom images, briefly
10 Looks dishonestly clueless, say
11 "You read me to filth"
12 Not worth celebrating
13 A whole load
14 Cook and Iger, for two
23 Chris Hadfield's former home: Abbr.
25 Airblade company
27 Virtue on the ice
28 Many Bandcamp offerings
30 "___ Auto" (old Volkswagen slogan)
31 What cashiers should be allowed to do on the job
32 "Fine, you're right"
33 Galaxy-brain individuals
35 Crams, say
38 See 31-Across
40 Forgive, on social media
42 Hit the big time
43 Las Vegas NFLer
46 Muscular
48 The product Lip Smackers, e.g.
49 ___ français (unlike this puzzle)
50 "Pfft, yeah right!"
51 Gen Z influencer JoJo
55 SoCal baseball team, on scoreboards

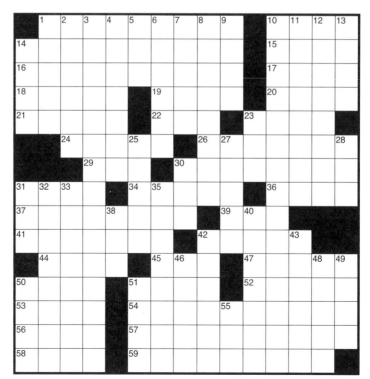

ANSWER, PAGE 96

1

```
E L E C T R O S W I N G
W A S T H A T S O H A R D
E S T R O G E N L E V E L S
  E L M E R   F A B   I L U
B Y E   S R I   R A P S O N
L A M B O S   D A Y R A T E S
O D E O N   W E L O S T
B A D U   B A N T U   O F F S
    T R A I T S   C O L O N
O B S T A C L E   M A T U R E
M O H A W K   O A R   I D K
G R U   F A M   P I P E D
  A N T I C A P I T A L I S T
  S U S H I B U R R I T O S
    T H E S A M E T O Y O U
```

2

```
M E M E P A G E S     S C O W
A R E Y O U O N E   N O H O W
P A N E L S H O W   A M A Z E
  S U M   L A S S   V A R Y
      A R A L     F A L L
C H O S E N F A M I L I E S
P A R K A   S T Y X   A S I S
U S A   D A I S I E S   I C E
S A L T   S E E M   E B I K E
  T H A N K S A M I L L I O N
    E T A S     O S L O
  H A T S   C A R T   N B C
V I L L A   A T T I C D O O R
I N T E L   S T A N D I N G O
A D H D     T A L K S E N S E
```

3

```
P O G O     B U Z Z E S U P
S H R U G   W A R I O W A R E
Y O U R E D A R N T O O T I N
    S T O N K S   S K I N S
U R L   S E T       R A E
B O O E D   P D F   C E L T
I A L R E A D Y H A V E
  D A R E R O L E M O D E L
    E P I S O D E R E C A P
M E L D   D E N     A D O R E
A Y O     B U C   N A P
H E M I N   A D A G I O
A L O T O F F I G H T L E F T
L I N T T R A P S   Y A X I S
O D D Y E A R S     F O R K
```

4

```
S T A C K   L O F I   W E S T
T A L O N   H U R T   C U K E
U N P R I V A T E D   S P I N
N D A   T A S T E     H A D
G E C S   N A A C P   W O R E
M A U I     L A Y E R E D
    B R I C K I P E D I A
  I M O V I E M U S I C
  O P E N I N G B A N D
I C A N S E E     O I N K
B A D U   S P E E D   T I N S
I N K   H E N R Y   P E I
S A I D   V I R T U A L P E T
E D D O   P L I E   N I L L A
S A S H   S E E R   G U E S T
```

5

```
O C S . . . T B S . I R K S
T R I P . P E R U . F E A T
T O G O . P A N E S . S A R I
A W H O L E L O T . . . D A N
W E T H E N O R T H . L O O K
A D S . A N O . Y O I N K S
. . U N S K I P P A B L E
. I N S T A P O E T R Y .
. H A G I A S O P H I A .
C E M E N T . T O E . G O V
R A W R . E X H A U S T I V E
A V O . . W O R S T E V E R
F E M A . M O N T E . X E R S
T H A N . O R E S . T U D E
S O N Y . O D D . . P M S
```

6

```
I B M . U N I T . . G M O
J O E F R E S H . . G R E W
E X T E N S I O N . S U I T E
S C A M . S T R I P M I N E S
T A P I R . . S C O O T .
. R U N O U T . D R A W M E
. Z I T C O M S . E R R O R
P I Z Z A B Y T H E S L I C E
U N L I T . S N I C K E T .
T E E N I E . . P O I S E D
. . G O T T A . T S A R S
M U C H N E E D E D . O B E Y
O D O R S . H A D I K N O W N
V O L T . . G I V E S O U T
E N D . . E T A L . K P H
```

7

```
F A N S . O G R E . S T O W
D R E A M T E A M . A T A R I
A T E F O R T W O . N I M B I
. E R A S E R . G L O S S
. M R T . P R Y . Y E S
A T A . I C U . . T H C
T A K E C E N T E R S T A G E
T H E N I C K M N E M O N I C
Y O U S A I D I T S I S T E R
. E S E . . R O T . E D U
. P M S . G P A . H E R
G A R B O . H A N S E L .
A T O L L . O S C A R B A I T
G L U E D . S T E P S O N T O
S A D S . T E S S . W A S P
```

8

```
S K A T E P U N K . A R I S E
O N S A L E N O W . M A R T A
L O S T M E D I A . A F R O S
I B E T . R O A M S . A I R Y
. S T E W . M E A D . G Y M
. D I V V Y . L E G A T O
V H S . P E S O S . F I T I N
W E L L E X C U U U U S E M E
B A A E D . O R G A N . D E Y
E L M E R S . F E E D S .
E T D . Y O G A . S U G A
T H A I . W A T T S . P R E P
L A N D S . T H E E M P I R E
E P C O T . W E N T A L L I N
S P E L L . A R T S T Y L E S
```

9

```
A H A B   D A L I       A F I
T O F U   E L E C T   C L A N
M O R T   W I N E O C L O C K
S P O T A D   T A G L I N E S
    S H I R K   X G A M E S
    A M O N G   L S A T
P A N T   P E R C E P T I V E
W H O S E   A A A   S E M I S
N I N J A E D I T S   N E A T
    B U R R   L E T M E
  B I S T R O   R E C U R
H I N T H I N T   P U T O U T
A D A M A N T I U M   R U S E
M E R E   G O T T O   A G E S
S T Y     P O E M   L E D S
```

10

```
O D D S   T H A T S C H I L L
L E N T   B A P E H O O D I E
A C A I   L I S T E N T O M E
F A L L C O L O R S     L E T
  L I L A C     A O K I
  B U S K E R   K I M C H I
M O R P H E M E S   A S H E S
U N A   R U I N G     E M I
S C R A P   S N O O T I E S T
H E Y N O W   S T O I C S
    A C H T     D E K E S
M S N     O H H E N R Y B A R
O N E T I M E U S E   P A V E
P A P E R S T R A W   O L E D
E G O T S T A T U S   O L D S
```

11

```
      D I E G O   A S A D A
    O P E N P O L Y C U L E S
A D V E N T C A L E N D A R S
L I E N S   O P I N E S
E R R S     T E E S     C F O
S E M A N A       C O E U R
    O N E T A K E W O N D E R
  G R O W N U P C E R E A L
H A R D T O S H O P F O R
O B O E S       T U F F E T
P E W     B R I E   M A T H
    P L A I N S   M A L T A
C O N S E R V A T I O N L A W
T H I S I S A W E N D Y S
V O L T A   L E E K S
```

12

```
M O O D B O A R D     G A T E
I M P R O V D U O   S E T U P
C A T E R E D T O   H O S T S
  R E V E R E   M A Y B E S O
    D I D I D O I T   L A I N
A M I L   T O R N A D O
T E N     N E G L E C T E D
M A T T E S     L I K E S O
S T O V E T O P S     A S L
      P L A N E T S   A L O E
P O S I   B E G E N T L E
A P C L A S S   E A R T A G
S T O O D   H I P P I E V A N
T I N T S   O R E O C R E M E
A C E S     T E N N E S S E E
```

13

```
S P I R I T   J O K E R A R C
P A M E L A   A D O R E Y O U
E S S A Y S   S O N G R E C S
A T O M S   E M M A   A S K S
K I D S M O V I E   A N I M E
E M O   R E N T A L   R E D
R E W I R E   E E V E E
  S N A I L S   R E X A L L
    M O S E S   R A T I O S
I R S   T E X A N S   F Y P
T E N T S   S L E E P W E A R
S T O W   S H U T   L I L L Y
S U R E S H O T   T O L I F E
A N T E L O P E   H Y E N A S
D E S T R E S S   A S S E N T
```

14

```
D S L     B F F   B S T O R Y
R E A L T R E E   O C U L A R
A S C I I A R T   D A D D Y S
T H I N M I N T   E L O
    C B D       G Y R A T E
    L O U   S K A     L I L
  W A L K A B L E C I T I E S
D I D N T S E E Y A T H E R E
A N Y S U G G E S T I O N S
R E D   A S K     S U S
E D I T O R       A D S
    I U D   R E L O A D E D
S K E T T I   I W A N N A G O
C O L A D A   R E M E D I A L
I S I N O N   I S O   S N L
```

15

```
T T Y L   P E A T   S N I T
O R E O C R E M E   Y O U S E
R U N S L O W O N   E L L I E
I T T E A M   R E C S   L T D
  H A Y S     T A N N I C
    O H M A N   T O O F A R
  Q U E E R E Y E   W I K I
F O U R D A Y W O R K W E E K
O W O W   L A T H E R E D
O N T A S K   S O R E R
  G A Y L I B     M E A N
J O B   O T I S   F L E W A T
I A L S O   G O P R I V A T E
B L E E P   I N G E N E R A L
E S S O   F E A T   N E L L
```

16

```
P U T R I D   C H A P L I N
A V E E N O   F U E L L I N G
P U P A T E   L E A D U P T O
E L I D E S   A S T O R
R A D A R   V I S U A L S
  N E U R O N   S L O O P
  C O S T A R     C O D E
W R I T T E N B Y A W O M A N
O A T H     L A R A M S
K N E E S   M A O I S M
  K D R A M A S   H U N C H
  B R E T T   B O N I T A
A N N O T A T E   A V I C I I
R E P O R T E D   N E T H E R
T U R K E Y S   D R Y E R S
```

17

```
POPSICLE   HIPPO
GREENDALE  INLAW
DEATHSTAR  STARE
NORTE SLIM ENID
   ERB COURTS
ADBREAKS TRIB
NEOS BUTTONMASH
EMO MYDEARS SUE
WOMBOCOMBO YELL
  EURO SUITEDUP
 ORDERS  LAS
CHAD NOON MILAN
RANIN OPERACAPE
URGES TEMPLATES
DESSA DOMENEXT
```

18

```
RFID    MINIBAR
ULTA  HOLOCENE
BAGS COOLBEANS
TIKI DARKSECRET
BEERMENUS LUC
ASSLOADS   BAKE
     DNI INTEGER
BENZENE MORSELS
BLOOMED PPE
BONO  ALIENATE
 SMH TRANSFLAG
DOTHETHING TWIG
ALOOCHAAT ABEL
RAPSKITS  ORSO
TVSTAND   LOTR
```

19

```
DEMIGOD LAUTNER
UBECAKE INPEACE
NOTABIT PITSTOP
EYELINER MASONS
 SOL GRANOLA
 REG SPORK VAT
MIDIS BOP BIRB
NOTIFICANHELPIT
POET GET SCOLD
RTS SORTS OWO
  EQUALTO DUG
MURMUR EARCANAL
INABIND IDARGUE
ROSERED NESTEGG
OSPREYS DRESSES
```

20

```
BESTED MEH  REF
RETIRE GRESCORE
IRONON MOCCASIN
SIR SIP SKABAND
KEEP MAC AMI
  BOI SAG ANA
DORITOSROULETTE
IWANNAGETBETTER
GENDERAFFIRMING
  DEV SOL TAC
  XEM RAP NSFW
FLYTRAP KOS PAR
LIVEINHD UPDATE
OVERSTAY TOUCAN
ESS  ATE STEELS
```

21

```
  B A A   A L T   S H E R O
  D A N G E R O U S W O M A N
C O N T E N T C R E A T O R S
R A D I O D I S N E Y   T I E
A B A   U S E         W I N T
B I G O T     F I T T I N G S
S T E P   P H I S H I N G
      E M A I L L I S T
      E R I T R E A N   E T S Y
A T T A C H E D   B R I T A
D E V S       P E I   L I L
R A O   W I S H I N G W E L L
E P I D E M I O L O G I S T S
P O L A R O P P O S I T E S
S T A V E   S I T   E S T
```

22

```
S A P P H I C   P A R S E C S
O C A N A D A   O N E P A R T
C A T G I R L   G A L A T E A
I C E   L I M E   C A R E E N
A I N T   S E X T O Y   R P G
L A T I N   D A W N   T I E S
      K E A   M I D T I E R
  C T R L Z   N A R C S
  D O O D L E S   S I T
W O N K   I S N T   G A M E S
I P S   C S T O R Y   C A S H
C R O N U T   B O O S   G P A
C O L O R I N   J U U L P O D
A M E R I C A   A R M O I R E
N O S I E S T   N E O P E T S
```

23

```
B O P I T     U N C L I P S
A R E N A   D A S H L I G H T
A C T I V   O M E L E T B A R
S A N T E   M I R   E I R E
  A I R P I R A T E   O M W
  I M A N E N I G M A   S A N
N E T   G O T R I C H
U S E D   S E E   H E A R
  S U B T L E R   L P S
R P G   C A R A M E L L O S
A L A   T R A D E D E A L
C A M I   C I N   A D O P T
E Y E S O C K E T   D O G I E
T O T A L M E S S   O P I N E
O N E Y E A R     N E A T S
```

24

```
S U B F O R S U B   E T S Y
E M A I L A P N E A   G A T E
W I I R E M O T E S   O K R A
S A L E S   N A R C   S E E R
U K E S   E G G S O N   T A N
P S Y   S U E   T O C O M E
    A I R B A G   R A G E D
  N O T T O O G O O D F O R
R O B O T   B E A N I E
U P S M E N   G E C   P A S
S E T   R E D O A K   V E S T
T S A R   W I K I   C I R C A
L O C O   E V A N H A N S E N
E U L A   R A P S I N G I N G
S T E M   S I T E S T A T S
```

25

```
L A S S I _ _ T H A _ _ T O K
A C T O N _ C L I N I C I A N
C H A N G _ H A N G S O N T O
K E I _ A V O I D _ A I G H T
_ D R U M U P B U S I N E S S
_ _ W H E E _ _ _ C D S _ _ _
F R A N C _ I N T O W _ D Y E
D O Y O U K N O W W H O I A M
A B S _ R U N T O _ A D E P T
_ _ A R R _ _ _ O T I S _ _ _
W I N G E D E Y E L I N E R
A N I O N _ M A T E S _ L E X
K I N G C O B R A _ A B O V E
E N J O Y M E N T _ I C I E R
S K A _ _ I D S _ _ D E L L S
```

26

```
J A W S _ E D A M _ _ A B I T
O H H I _ B E T A S _ C R A W
T H A T S A F A C T _ N U D E
_ _ T I N Y _ R O E _ E S M E
P L A N A _ _ I S P Y _ H I T
H A M _ P S P _ G O G E T
I T I T S P R O N O U N S
_ E Y E S L I K E A H A W K
_ O S H A V I O L A T I O N
T U T U S _ _ S S T _ T B A
B R R _ T H U S _ E T H O S
G O M E _ P T A _ P I A F
A J A R _ A U D I O T R A C K
M A I A _ D R I P S _ O M N I
E N D S _ _ N E A T _ T E N T
```

27

```
G R A B B E D A F E W Z S
R O L L E D I C E C R E A M
A T E A F U L L T H I N G O F
Y E S N O _ _ C O N G E A L
_ _ C R U T C H _ G A R R Y
L A P _ E Z R A _ F I R
A C A I _ B A R T E N D E R S
S T A N L E Y _ R A G E D O N
T I K T O K S T A R _ N E M O
_ _ E N S _ H I E S _ N E W
A W A R D _ C A T D O G
P A N D O R A _ _ N O S E D
T R A I N I N G M O N T A G E
_ N I C E T O E M E E T Y O U
_ S T R E E T A R T I S T S
```

28

```
B L O T _ L U V _ _ G O H A M
F I R E M A R I O _ S L O M O
F L E X I N G O N _ A D V I L
L O S A N G E L E S _ P E S T
_ _ S O U S _ _ T S A R S
B A R B R A _ S P O I L S
A G A B _ G A M I N G _ O B I
J A C Q U E L I N E N O V A K
A R E _ H A T T E R _ C E D E
_ C O U R S E _ C I T R U S
_ Y A C H T _ T O R O
G U R U _ S E S A M E B E E F
A M B L E _ S O M E N E R V E
S M E A R _ E P I D E R M I S
H Y D R A _ S L Y _ S A L T
```

29

```
HOVER ■ STATUSBAR
ABIDE ■ AEROSPACE
SARAH ■ LEAVEOPEN
UMAMIBOMB ■ CREST
PAL ■ RAN ■ CAT
■ TPED ■ BLURSDAY
■ OWLS ■ GUATEMALA
ICEE ■ DORKS ■ ORBS
CHEAPDATE ■ EDNA
HOTSHOTS ■ FRET
■ ETS ■ IOU ■ OST
SNIDE ■ NUDEPHOTO
TACOSHELL ■ TITAN
IDONTBITE ■ EFILE
RANTSONAS ■ DINED
```

30

```
LONGFURBY ■ BASTA
ONEORMORE ■ ALTOS
BIGDIPPER ■ STOIC
BOA ■ ASEA ■ NICOLE
ENTER ■ STAYSOPEN
DYED ■ HIHAT ■ MITT
■ ITONYA ■ RENTS
DOTOO ■ BADGE
SIPON ■ MEMOJI
IGER ■ TONED ■ ARMS
MINIONESE ■ ONEIL
POPART ■ URNS ■ PSA
FRILL ■ LIKELIEST
ONTWO ■ ATARIGAME
ROSEN ■ DETONATES
```

31

```
SHOWIN ■ PREWASH
YEAHSO ■ DOADANCE
SYRIAN ■ ONMEDIUM
■ TWODOZEN ■ MLA
EPEE ■ IMIN ■ CAPN
COLLIDES ■ COLT
ONLINESCHOOL
■ DELIVERYROOMS
■ INSTOREPROMO
SEEK ■ LUSTSFOR
BUDS ■ HILL ■ WOLE
UBI ■ HACIENDA
MASTODON ■ CATSPA
PROPPING ■ ARCHES
SUNSETS ■ ATHENS
```

32

```
■ WILDE ■ SWAM ■ LGA
SENORA ■ CALAMARI
TIGGER ■ ONELITER
ARROWS ■ NEXTSTEP
TDISC ■ OED ■ ALITO
SOD ■ ASH ■ ACED
■ TROYANDABED
SHEBELIEVED
GRAYASEXUAL
VEIN ■ ESL ■ OGS
ATLAS ■ LID ■ AMNOT
COATEDON ■ UNABLE
ANNOTATE ■ MCCAFE
YUKSITUP ■ PHASER
SPA ■ NEST ■ SEWED
```

33

```
P R E H R T   . C O O L O F F
B O X I E R   . C O N T I N U E
S T A N C E   . H O T S A L S A
  . I M G O N N A G O . M I S S
  . P E N T O O L . . N Y T
B A L D . U S E S . T E E S
A R E A M A N . R I V E R A
Z E S T E R . W I S E T O
  . Y E E T E D L A S T F E W
C O N S . S A D E . P E R L
O U T . D E A D A I R .
I D E S . B A R N A C L E S
N O N O G R A M . S T O N E D
O N C A M E R A . H O T C A R
P E E R S A T . I N S E T S
```

34

```
G O S T A G   . G L U E D T O
A N T H R O   . I R O N G R I P
B A R E S T   . M I N D G A M E
. W A Y . S N E E Z E . G E D
T H I R S T E D F O R . O R S
W I N E M O M . T H U S
S M S . I N E A R S H O T
. B R E A K O P E N
. B A N D N A M E S . A B I
A U T O . P L E A D E D
A S S . F A L S E L A S H E S
S L C . F L A I R S . S E L
K E E P I T P G . O S I R I S
M E M E C O I N . U R G E N T
E P I P E N S . T I N D E R
```

35

```
I T C A M E . U P S . N O W
D E L T A S . T A O . O N O
E L A S T I G I R L . E V E R
A L I . E C T O P L A S M
S E R B . S T A Y . R E P
. R O U T E R . R E M I N D
. S W E E T R E V E N G E
K E E P O N K E E P I N G O N
O M G A H I T T W E E T
D I G S O N . I N W A R D
. C S U . C A R T . L U I S
Q U E E R C O R E . S R I
U R L S . A C I D W A S H E D
A S L . L O S . E N T I C E
Y A S . F A E . T A U N T S
```

36

```
H A N D S T A M P . S A T I N
D R O O L O V E R . U T I C A
T E T E A T E T E . P I L E S
V W S . B E R G . L E S T E
S E E D . T A P I R S
E G R E S S . L A P S U P
T O I L E T . A I R L E A K
S O O . T O K . L E O . P A D
. D U B I O U S . A M P E R E
. S A N G R E . D O D R A G
. U S E D L P . A M O R
D E B T S . F E S T . A K A
J E L L O . W I S E A C R E S
A L L E N . A S T E R O I D S
B L A S E . P O O P E M O J I
```

37

```
B U G   ■   K I M I   ■   M O A T S
O P E N M I C E R   ■   A P N E A
A S Y O U W E R E   ■   E A T E N
T E S T S I T E   ■ ■   L I N T
E X E R T S   ■   K F C   ■   G M A
L Y R E   ■   H A V E I D E A S
■ ■   D E C O D E R R I N G
■   R A D I C A L A C T S
■   H O M E S K I L L E T   ■
S I L E N C E R S   ■   O B O E
A T L   ■   S O Y   ■   G A M I N G
Y M C A   ■   V I L L A G E R
Y E A S T   ■   R I D E O R D I E
E U L E R   ■   S C E N E K I D S
S P L A Y   ■   S E E N   ■   G A S
```

38

```
A W E S O M E   ■   P B A N D J S
P I P E D I N   ■   H I D E O U T
C R I T I C S   ■   O T H E L L O
L E T   ■   E R U P T E D   ■   P I P
A T O P   ■   O R E O S   ■   T H A I
S A M O A   ■   E P A   ■   P R I N T
S P E N D S   ■   S P R A I N
■   C I T Y   ■   P E E P
■   S H E R O S   ■   F A L T E R
G O Y O U   ■   U W U   ■   N E H R U
I N N S   ■   P L A N B   ■   D I O N
B E A   ■   W A L T Z I N   ■   S T D
L I P K I T S   ■   I Z O M B I E
E S S E N C E   ■   P E T M I C E
T H E Y S H E   ■   S T E M G A P
```

39

```
A L F R E D   ■   F D A   ■   I S S A
N O R E L A T I O N   ■   O P A L
T R A V E L B L O G   ■   M O T T
S E T   ■   C L A M M Y   ■   O R B S
■ ■   S T A R E   ■   I T T Y
C O W E R S   ■   D E P T H S
C H E M O   ■   S O R E S   ■   B O Y
T H E I N F I N I T Y S A G A
V I D   ■   I O W A N   ■   O I L E R
■   N O C R A P   ■   H U L L E D
■   T U B A   ■   O P A R T
S I M S   ■   L A T E S T   ■   C B C
W A B E   ■   U M A C T U A L L Y
A R E S   ■   G E T S E R I O U S
M A R S   ■   E N O   ■   A N D Y E T
```

40

```
S N A P S S H U T   ■   I N K S
T O R O N T O S I X   ■   C A N I
I H A V E A N A M E Y K N O W
M O B   ■   E Y E   ■   O N E I O T A
■   B T W   ■   N O S E   ■
■   L O C A L S   ■   N E S S I E
■   B A T H R O O M   ■   S T A T S
W E S   ■   M S P E C   ■   T M I
W A S P S   ■   S U G A R P I E
E M O R A P   ■   P A L A C E
■   O R E O   ■   C C S
S H A P I R O   ■   D U E   ■   N I P
H I G H S C H O O L D R A M A
I S E E   ■   Y O U T U B E L A G
P S S T   ■   K I S S Y F A C E
```

41

C	U	D	I		L	E	S	S				C	I	A
A	H	E	M		E	V	O	K	E		V	A	N	S
T	O	M	S		M	A	N	I	A		A	R	C	S
	H	O	T	F	U	D	G	E	S	U	N	D	A	E
		E	I	R	E		D	E	S	I	R	E	S	
P	E	D	A	L	S				S	A	L	E	M	S
S	M	E	L	T		A	C	L	U		L	A	P	
L	O	F	I	H	I	P	H	O	P	R	A	D	I	O
	J	I	N		D	E	E	P		O	P	E	R	A
D	I	N	G	U	S				T	O	U	R	E	R
S	P	I	T	S	A	T		S	E	N	D			
H	E	T	H	E	Y	O	F	T	H	E	D	A	Y	
A	D	I	A		S	P	E	A	R		I	W	O	N
R	I	O	T		O	U	T	T	A		N	O	D	E
P	A	N				P	E	E	N		G	O	A	T

42

C	A	R	D		M	A	G	I				P	M	S
A	L	E	R	T		A	M	O	S		G	R	I	N
R	A	D	I	O	E	D	I	T	S		L	O	N	I
O	N	A	V	E	R	A	G	E		S	O	P	U	P
L	O	N	E		A	T	O	M		T	W	O	T	E
E	N	T	R	Y				S	A	S	S	E	D	
			S	E	A	S	H	A	N	T	I	E	S	
		A	L	L	P	R	O	N	O	U	N	S		
		D	R	I	P	P	I	N	G	W	E	T		
P	E	A	C	E	S				S	H	E	G	O	
U	M	B	E	R		S	T	A	T		E	C	O	N
R	E	I	N	S		P	O	L	K	A	D	O	T	S
I	R	A	S		M	A	N	G	O	L	A	S	S	I
N	I	N	E		A	R	E	A		F	R	I	E	D
A	T	S			C	E	D	E		K	A	T	E	

43

K	O	K	O	M	O		A	C	R	E	S			
H	A	U	L	I	N		L	O	U	D	E	R		
A	T	R	E	S	T		S	O	N	G	R	E	C	
N	Y	T		M	I	A		L	I	E		G	A	S
			C	A	P	T	A	I	N		R	I	T	A
	G	O	T	T	A	G	O		R	E	S	E	T	
	D	A	D	C	O	R	E		S	E	N	T	R	A
S	A	M	E	H	E	I	G	H	T	P	A	R	T	Y
A	R	M	I	E	S		A	Y	Y	L	M	A	O	
S	T	A	N	D		A	T	E	L	I	E	R		
H	I	R	E		W	E	E	N	I	E	S			
A	N	A		P	I	G		A	S	S		L	I	P
	G	Y	R	A	T	E	D		T	A	K	E	T	O
	S	U	L	T	A	N		I	L	I	V	E	D	
	N	S	Y	N	C		C	L	A	I	M	S		

44

U	M	A	M	I	B	O	M	B		V	A	S	E	S
M	O	D	E	R	A	T	O	R		I	W	U	V	U
P	R	O	T	O	S	T	A	R		N	O	P	E	S
S	T	S		N	E	O	N		P	E	L	E		
			C	A	L	M		C	I	S		R	E	A
		I	R	L		A	L	A	S			F	M	L
O	N	E	L	I	N	E	R	C	O	M	I	C	S	
T	H	E	M	O	S	T	O	R	E	O	O	R	E	O
H	A	V	E	Y	O	U	N	O	S	H	A	M	E	
A	N	I			B	R	I	T		A	T	S		
W	A	T		E	E	K		B	E	N	S			
	A	R	I	L		L	A	N	D		S	N	L	
G	O	B	A	G		T	I	C	T	A	C	T	O	E
F	I	L	T	H		E	L	O	R	A	T	I	N	G
S	L	E	E	T		T	I	N	Y	H	O	M	E	S

45

```
T V S P E C I A L S █ A B B Y
W I T H T O N G U E █ F R E E
I N R E A L T I M E █ L O L A
S T O W █ D O T E █ O A S I S
T A M █ █ N A N T U C K E T █
E G A D █ C A T S I T █ I V Y
D E E P N O T E █ A R I S E █
█ █ A O N E █ B R A N █ █ █ █
█ H A D N T █ S E A P O R T S
P E R █ G R A T E S █ T E R I
A L M A M A T E R █ █ S I N █
S L O M O █ H A M M █ U P O N
S I R I █ C O M E I N S I D E
U S E S █ A M E N S I S T E R
P H D S █ R E D U C T R E S S
```

46

```
█ █ B I T I N G S A R C A S M
█ B O D Y N E U T R A L I T Y
W A R M E D E M U P F O R Y A
A L O E █ I D S █ E T S █ █ █
T E N D I E S █ C G I E D █ █
█ █ █ Y D S █ S I G N S O N █
E B O O K █ S P R I G █ N A P
S U L U █ G E I C O █ S O D A
T O M █ N E M E A █ S T R A W
█ Y E S I T I S █ M A I █ █ █
█ C L A S S █ P A Y M E N T █
█ █ I G A █ M E H █ M A U I █
A R O M A T H E R A P I S T S
P A P E R A I R P L A N E S █
E N T R A N C E S O N G S █ █
```

47

```
U P L I F T █ P C S █ E T C H
R O O M I E █ S A T I R I Z E
N T U P L E █ S P A C E M A N
█ █ R E M █ T O R E █ E R S █
█ G O T █ █ S E T U P █ █ █ █
█ H E P █ M C S █ O N E S █ █
H A T E T O E A T A N D R U N
A L F R E D O L I N G U I N I
D A R U D E S A N D S T O R M
█ L O S T █ D E S █ I D A █ █
█ M E A L S █ █ █ I F S █ █ █
S P A █ L E O S █ G N U █ █ █
K A T A K A N A █ A D L I B S
I P O D S K I N █ W I L S O N
T A B S █ S A D █ P A Y P A L
```

48

```
D I P L O M A T S █ █ D O R A
O K H E R E S O N E █ E R A S
I N S T A N T W I N █ B O P S
T E C S █ D A N D D █ T U B E
A W A I T █ █ S E I S █ R E N
L I L N A S X █ T U S K E D █
L T E █ P A R I S █ C H E F S
█ █ H E W A S L I K E █ █ █ █
M O W E R █ Y O U R E █ M V P
E H E H E H █ E A R H A I R █
A R E █ D O O F █ S E N S E █
L O A D █ S W I R L █ A D A M
K U B O █ E L L I O T P A G E
I G O R █ D E E P R O O T E D
T H O M █ T R A N S N E S S █
```

49

```
A L L W E T . . G R A M P A
G E O R G E . . R O O M B A S
E N S I G N . B A D U M T S S
N O T T O O F A R . T A I T O
C R O S S R I B . S E N T I N
Y E N . . . L Y F E . Y M A
. . M Y D M S A R E O P E N
A C C R U E S I N T E R E S T
T R A S H K E T B A L L . .
T A L . E T T A . . A L A
E V A D E S . E S C O O T E R
M A M A S . D R E A M T E A M
P L A N T E R S . P A T A K I
T H R E E V E . O N E S I E
S O I S E E . . S I R E N S
```

50

```
K I T . . E S P . M A P L E
E N O S . C A L I . A L O O F
I T M E . A T O N . R O W L F
T R A N S T I M E L I N E S .
H O T D O G T O A S T E R .
. S O D O I . P D A . O P T
. . O N R A M P . L M F A O
E W W W . L U L L S . I F S O
S A I N T . S P E C K S .
C P R . O N T . A L T A R
. E S P O R T S L E A G U E
. A L L S T A R W E E K E N D
C H E A P . L I O N . E G O S
H A S T O . I N R E . S A N E
A S S E T . A I D . . P S L
```

51

```
T H I R S T F O R . T H A N K
H O M O P H O N E . A U L I I
I N I T I A L E D . T B O N D
N O T . E T D . S H E S H E D
. L A N D S . B E E R . A R O
C U T E . S T E A L T H .
F L I E S O U T . L O E W
S U N D O W N . C O T T A G E
. G L U E . P A S S E S O N
. E P I C U R E . R A T E
M M E . B R A N . A D O B O
A I R P O D S . R T E . I S P
S C R E W . B E A T T A P E S
T R O L L . A P P L E P E E L
S O R T S . H A T E R E A D S
```

52

```
F E R B . . B I G A S S
O P E R A . C Y N I C A L
R S L A S H . P O T E N T L Y
. I S I T T R U E . S A I D
C L A S S T R I P . S E O
F I N . P A D L O C K I N G
O U T T A V E E R L E F T
. I S P E P S I O K .
. C A N I P L A Y . P E S O S
D E B A T E B R O S . A P P
I R S . L A G U A R D I A
A T O B . S O D A S H O P
B A L L C A G E . S O S O O N
L I V E I N S . Y E S N O
O N E D G E . . S T E W
```

53

```
H A L   M A S T   M E G A
T R I   M A C H O   E A R L S
M I N C E M E A T   T R A C E
L A K O T A   M E G A N F O X
    E K E S   E M I L   F A T
  B D E           S H U I
A R I Z O N A G R E E N T E A
V I N E C O M P I L A T I O N
I M P R O V C O M E D I A N S
    R O T I         D R S
P T O   I C E S   S L I T
R U F F L E U P   H O E I N G
E G I R L   R E H E A R S E D
P A L E O   O C E A N   T S A
    T E E S   S K Y R   S T Y
```

54

```
G A Z E D   P F U N K   A C E
A L I F E   R E P A I R M A N
L A T I N   I N S I D E O U T
      C L O W N C A R   M U S E
    P R I V A T E D   F I N E R
L I E N O R   A G E N T S
S N A G   R A V I O L I
D E M   F I L M S E T   D A M
      T W O D A Y S   C A F E
    I C H I R O   B E A T E N
S C R E W   G S T A R R A W
N Y A N   S U M O D O J O
I S T H E A C O N   D A N Z A
F E E L S I C K Y   E C L A T
F A R   P L I E S   S K Y P E
```

55

```
W A T C H I T   B A R B S
A T E L O C A L   O C E A N
R A P O P E R A S   D I D S O
T R I S   T E S T R I D E S
S I D E B   T R I E S F O R
    G U S T   U M S   I O U
    B A L L H O G S   I N N S
I F I M B E I N G H O N E S T
P A G E   P R E L O V E D
A C L   E T S   E T A L
D E E P N O T E   L E A S E
  P A R T N E R U P   G R I D
M A G E E   D I D A D A N C E
B L U E R   N O N U N I O N
A M E N S   N E A T E N S
```

56

```
B U D L I G H T   G I G I
U S E A S B A I T   O H M A N
N H L P L A Y E R   L O T S O
T E R S E   D R O N E S H O T
S R I   I N S T A   T E L
  S O F A R   H O T O I L
    A R I A N A   D O N N A
T H I S I S H A L L O W E E N
O U N C E   I M T O R N
P G F I L M   I S S U E
  G O N   O V E N S   P A W
B A D A S S E R Y   B A R G E
A B U T S   R U M O R M I L L
E L M E R   A P P R A I S E D
Z E P S   T H E D R E S S
```

57

S	O	D	A	S	T	R	E	A	M		S	P	A	R
I	N	V	I	T	E	O	N	L	Y		H	U	L	A
M	A	D	R	E	S	P	E	C	T		E	T	O	N
			P	E	T	E	R	O	U	T		I	N	D
	A	W	O	L			G	A	R	B	A	N	Z	O
S	L	I	D	E	S	B	Y		N	O	G	M	O	S
I	O	N	S		P	A	C	T		N	E	O		
P	E	G		C	A	R	O	U	S	E		T	A	B
	S	Z	A		I	M	B	I		J	I	L	T	
P	A	P	E	R	S		P	A	T	R	I	O	T	S
O	P	E	N	B	E	T	A			U	M	N	O	
M	O	C		S	L	I	N	G	I	N	K			
P	L	I	E		F	A	I	R	U	S	E	L	A	W
O	L	A	Y		I	N	E	E	D	A	R	I	D	E
M	O	L	E		E	A	S	Y	S	T	R	E	E	T

58

L	O	G	O	F	F		M	A	S		D	D	S	
I	R	A	N	A	I	R		A	N	I	M	O	J	I
B	E	S	E	E	C	H		K	I	T	E	M	A	N
			M	O	R	S	E		E	L	A	T	I	N	G
P	R	O	F	S		A	M	P		R	A	N	G	E
S	E	N	T			E	R	R		P	O	O	R	
I	V	E	H	A	D	E	N	O	U	G	H			
	Y	O	G	A	S	T	U	D	I	O	S			
	S	O	U	T	H	D	E	T	R	O	I	T		
C	A	P	E		B	R	O				I	N	C	H
A	C	I	D	S		A	L	A		M	C	G	E	E
R	E	L	A	T	E	D		S	H	E	A	R		
A	D	E	Y	E	M	I		M	E	D	L	E	Y	S
D	I	O	S	M	I	O		R	A	I	L	C	A	R
S	T	N		S	T	L			D	A	Y	S	P	A

59

C	A	M	E	A	T		W	H	A	T	A	G	E	T
U	R	A	N	I	A		O	O	H	S	P	I	C	Y
D	I	E	T	R	C		M	E	G	A	F	L	O	P
			I	H	O	P	E	S	O		R	E	L	O
		A	C	U	M	E	N		T	H	E	S	I	S
I	M	V	E	G	A	N		I	C	O	N			
M	A	I			N	I	G	H	T	C	O	R	E	
A	R	A	B		S	A	M	S	A		H	O	A	X
C	A	N	Y	O	U	N	O	T			P	G	A	
			D	E	B	T		O	P	O	S	S	U	M
R	A	T	E	D	M		P	R	E	P	P	Y		
A	S	O	S		I	N	A	Y	E	A	R			
S	P	R	I	N	T	E	D		S	Q	U	I	R	M
P	E	T	G	A	T	O	R		H	U	N	T	E	R
S	C	E	N	E	O	N	E		Y	E	G	O	D	S

60

	S	M	S		M	B	A		R	E	C	S	
U	T	A	H		Y	E	S		I	P	A	I	D
N	A	C	H	O	H	A	T		C	O	R	R	I	E
O	R	E		X	E	N	O	G	E	N	D	E	R	S
	A	D	V	E	R	B		A	B	Y	S	S	E	S
K	N	O	W	Y	O	U	R	M	E	M	E			
R	I	N	S	E		R	A	I	L		T	W	I	N
A	S	I		S	P	R	I	N	T	S		I	N	E
B	E	A	T		R	I	N	G		P	A	G	E	R
			A	L	O	T	S	C	H	A	N	G	E	D
S	P	O	K	E	T	O		H	E	R	A	L	D	
V	I	D	E	O	E	S	S	A	Y	S		E	M	O
U	N	I	O	N	S		T	I	D	E	P	O	O	L
	G	U	N	I	T		O	R	A		S	U	R	E
	M	E	D	S		P	S	Y		A	T	E		

61

```
T B D . D A T E . . . . S A C
H I E . E V E N T . . I K I D
E T C . V A N D W E L L E R S
A T O P . E L I L I L L Y .
. E R R O R M E S S A G E . .
G R A I N I E S T . R O T C .
L A T V I A N S . . . T O L D
A L I . T N T . S A T . N E O
D E V I . . A T Y P I C A L
. S E C T . P L A Y E R O N E
. G E O M E T R Y D A S H .
. R O A D C R E W . S T A B
F A U X O U T R A G E . U N O
O G R E . . H E R E S . M D S
B E D . . D S E S . E S C
```

62

```
M A C S . A F I . T E S T S
F L A K . P O W E R H O U S E
W I K I . P R O T E I N B A R
. M E T H . M U T E S . S P F
G O P O O F . L U L L . I R S
I N A W O R L D . . L A S E
G Y N . D O I N G A B I T .
. B O O K T U B E R .
. V E R T E B R A E . A S P
N A A N . E L S A G A T E
W A N . A B U T . E S H A R P
A T E . M A N O R . Y O G I
L I S T E N I N O N . S A V E
L O S I N G T I M E . T M E N
E N A C T . . T E D . S E N D
```

63

```
. . . S T R I V E . G M A J O R
. C A R O L E R . R E C E D E
N O T I C I N G . O R A T E D
S L I N K E D . B U R S T S .
F O R K E D . P O N Y T A .
W R I E R . H O L D M E .
P A C T . E A T T H E R I C H
I D A . M X M T O O N . C H O
C O L L A P S I N G . J E A N
. . E M O T E S . C E L L O
. . C E A S E S . H O T A I R
. S O C C E R . F I N A N C E
A L O H A S . C O N F I D E D
S O R E S T . A T T I M E S
L E S S S O . P O S T E R
```

64

```
S A W B U C K S . C I T I
A T T H I S H O U R . A T O N
L Y R I C V I D E O . K E P I
A L I T . S C A M S . E R I N
S E A . I T A K E I T B A C K
. . . N A H . . N E A T
T V C A M E R A S . A T I E R
B I A S . M A G I C . T O T E
S A T I N . J O B A G E N C Y
. A G E S . . B R R .
I M L O S I N G Y O U . A U G
D I O R . T U R O W . A C N E
I N G E . O K A Y A T B E S T
N O U N . N E P O B A B I E S
G R E G . D E S O L A T E
```

65

```
I N T W O . F I N . . . S A G
P A R E U . O N E . A P P L Y
S H E E T . R A W . S U R E R
. . B U S . T W E R K H E R O
B R U N O . H E R E . L E T S
L A C . U A E . . D O E . .
T S H I R T W E A T H E R . .
. P E T C H I M P A N Z E E .
. T H E L I S T G O E S O N
. . E S E . . R S S . T I E
I T M E . T E C H . E Y I N G
G R E W W E A R Y . C A N .
P U R E E . S A M . O H G O D
A C I D S . E V E . N O O N E
Y E T . . L E S . D O N T S
```

66

```
M A P . . P E T S . I M I N
A C E . R I V A L . C O N A N
C O N C I S E L Y . Y O B R O
O R A L B . R E D S . T O U S
S N L A L U M . O H O . X T C
. . W E B O U G H T A Z O O
B S M E T E R S . . T W E R P
R U E D . R E A C H . T R U E
I S T A N . G R Y P H O N S
T H A T S T H E I D E A . .
T I L . A L E . T E N N E R S
A B L E . C A R E . D K R A P
N O I C E . L A R G E S O D A
Y A C H T . T R I E D . D A M
. T A O S . H E A T . E R S
```

67

```
A N Y . I W I S H . A L I S T
W O E . C A N W E . L O T T O
E T S . U N P I N . L O S E S
I A M A . N U G . V I T A L S
G R A B S A T . S I N . B L U
H O N C H O . S I R . C L A P
. . D A R K E S T H O U R
. . G E N D E R Q U E E R
. G I F K E Y B O A R D
T O F U . R E S . L E I D A Y
R O T . H I S . I T S T I M E
E D I S O N . T K O . S L U E
M O D E L . M I N U S . A L T
O N E N D . S N O R T . T E E
R E A D S . N E W S Y . E T D
```

68

```
S A L A D B A R S . . S A P S
E P I C M O V I E . S L U R P
W A N T S P E T S . H O T E L
O C K . T E E S . R E U S E
N E I L . O N S I T E . M S N
. . N E A T O . O A K . N O D
. . T B H . N I R V A N A
. D A M I E N . S N A I L S
P A L E T T E . T V S . .
A T L . S O P . D E E T S
Y E N . T P O S E D . A I M S
S L I C E . T A I L . D U A
T I G R E . I N C O R R E C T
U N H I P . S T E V E A O K I
B E T S . . M A D E S E N S E
```

69

```
T S K . . C A P O . . I N S T A
O P A H . . O L A V . . T O T A L
M A T E I N T W O . . O S A K A .
. S I L K S O N I C . . E Y E S .
. . A L E C . . D R A B S . . . .
. . N A I L S . . Y A L L S . . .
B O B O . O O O . S N E A K S . .
Y O U W O U L D N T G E T I T . .
E N T E R S . A B A . D E N Y . .
. A T W A R . S A L E S . . . . .
. . D O L A N . . P R E P . . . .
S H I N . P O S T E R A R T . . .
L O A T H . K P O P S T A N S . .
I L L G O . I U D S . S W I M . .
D Y S O N . A N D I . N A H . . .
```

70

```
. . . . G E O B L O C K E D . .
. . . C O F F E E S H O P A U .
. . A F F I L I A T E L I N K S
. L A L A L A N D . R A C I E R
. A R T S E T . . . . . T E S S
. M O E T . E S P O U S A L . .
. A N A . . C A R N A L . . . .
. . M L G M O N T A G E S . . .
. . A A A R G H . . . E P A . .
. . W I S H E S O N . M E A T .
I D E D . . . . O L E O L A . .
D A R I N G . R E S E R V E D .
O N E T O A C U S T O M E R . .
. G O O D L I S T E N E R . . .
. K N E E D E E P I N . . . . .
```

71

```
. I N E V E R N O T I C E D .
. O N E M O R E E P I S O D E .
T H E T O N I G H T D O U G H .
R I F T S . C A R E Y . R E O .
I S L E . . I U D . S T I R . .
L E A D D O W N . G L E N N . .
L E T . A S H E S . E I D . . .
. . B L O O D T E S T . . . . .
. . L E E . S C A R S . T B A .
C L O N K . O R E O T H I N . .
H O N E . B A N . H W A T . . .
O R G . M I S T Y . L E A S E .
S E A S O N P R E M I E R E S .
E N G I N E C O O L A N T S . .
N E O N A T A L W A R D S . . .
```

72

```
. R A I S E C A I N . F A S T
C O L D P L U N G E . E C H O
E Y E B O M B I N G . I C A N
O A K E N . A M I S . G U M S
S L E D S . N E T . I N R E .
. . G O O D S . I T S S A F E
. . W R Y . D O E S I T U P .
S I G N . S W A N S . G E L S
I C E F L O E S . S U N . . .
T O N O E N D . M A N O R . .
. N I R O . G B A . B R A G S
A C U T . S E E K . L A I L A
S E S H . I S E E L O N D O N
I D E A . W I F I A C C E S S
F E S T . A N Y T A K E R S .
```